TEXAS ETHNIC CUISINE
CUISINE
STIRRING THE POT

By Dianna Hunt

GREAT TEXAS LINE PRESS

THE AUTHOR

Dianna Hunt is a longtime journalist and native Texan who has lived in virtually every corner of the state, from North Texas to South Texas and from deep East Texas to the West. Her propensity to stop and look around while driving the back roads of Texas has introduced her to the lively ethnic cultures still at work in the Lone Star State. She's an award-winning journalist who has worked for some of the largest and smallest newspapers in Texas — the *Houston Chronicle*, the *Dallas Morning News* and the *Fort Worth Star-Telegram* among them — and as co-owner of a weekly newspaper in Central Texas.

Cover photos by Ralph Lauer
Book and cover design by Jared Stone
Edited by Amy Culbertson

© Great Texas Line Press

Bulk sales of books from Great Texas Line Press are available at special discounts for fund raising, promotions and premiums.

Great Texas Line Press
P.O. Box 11105
Fort Worth, Texas 76110
1-800-73TEXAS / Fax 817-926-0420
greattexas@hotmail.com
www.greattexasline.com

Great Texas Line Press strives to be a socially conscious publishing house. A portion of proceeds from several books is donated to worthy causes around the state, including Habitat for Humanity of Fort Worth, North Fort Worth Historical Society, Texas Dance Hall Inc. of Austin, and Big Bend Educational Foundation of Terlingua. Every effort is made to produce our books in Texas by family-run printing companies and to engage Texas writers, photographers, designers, illustrators and editors forced out of daily journalism by the newspaper industry crisis.

A STEP BACK IN TIME

A DRIVE THROUGH TEXAS can take you on a cultural journey through the state's heritage. Step into a restaurant or bakery in the Central Texas town of West, and you'll almost certainly find Czech kolaches and sausage. East Texas is the place for soul-food classics like sweet potato pie. Spend some time in San Antonio, and you'll encounter chiles rellenos and tres leches cake.

In Bosque County near Waco, you'll find Norwegian treats on Constitution Day in May, or you can drive south to Panna Maria for a taste of the state's Polish heritage. A trip through the Texas Hill Country in the fall will introduce you to descendants of the German settlers, who still celebrate Oktoberfest with sausage, polka bands and beer.

Visit the Alabama-Coushatta reservation in the Big Thicket near Livingston or the Tigua tribe near El Paso to experience native culture. Head to southeast Texas around Beaumont and Port Arthur for some Cajun entertainment on Mardi Gras, or for boudin sausage at smokehouses and filling stations any time of year.

Certainly many other cultures are reflected in modern-day Texas: the Vietnamese and Laotian communities around Houston and in other large cities, the Italians and Greeks who settled in Galveston and northward, the Wendish people near Giddings in Lee County, the Arab and Indian communities sprouting up in urban areas, to name only a few. Many of these have made their marks on Texas' cuisine — in southeast Texas, the phenomenon of Vietnamese-owned restaurants cooking Cajun seafood staples such as crawfish is a textbook example of the culinary melting pot.

But the communities reflected in this book defined the geographic areas where they settled in early Texas in unique ways that endure today. We chose them because the descendants of those immigrants have kept their culture alive in the places where they live, so that each of those places is indelibly marked by — and identified with — their ethnic legacy. They love their heritage and honor their ancestors by continuing those traditions in the foods they cook. Here's a sampling.

—DIANNA HUNT

CONTENTS

NORWEGIAN TEXANS: LUTEFISK AND LEFSE   28

CZECH TEXANS: KOLACHES AND BUCHTAS   38

MEXICAN TEXANS: THE ROOTS OF TEX-MEX   49

NATIVE TEXANS: FRY BREAD AND HOMINY

THE HISTORY OF NATIVE AMERICANS IN TEXAS is a mix of cultures. Before the white settlers arrived, some tribes, such as the Comanches in West and Central Texas, were nomadic, relying on foods they killed or gathered along the way. Others, including the Caddos in East Texas, had a farming culture. The Pueblo Indians in far West Texas near El Paso lived much as their village-dwelling relatives did in New Mexico and Arizona. Today, there are three federally recognized tribes in Texas: the Alabama-Coushatta in the Big Thicket area near Livingston, the Tiguas at the Ysleta del Sur near El Paso and the Kickapoo near Eagle Pass. Their traditional foods, like their culture, draw from those who came before them, and from the commodities — flour, beans, cheese — they were given as they moved onto tribal lands, some as early as the late 1800s or early 1900s.

INDIAN FRY BREAD

Fry bread developed on reservations as a way for Native Americans to feed their families with the government commodities — typically flour and lard — they were given. If you had beans and cheese, too, you could make tacos. Today fry bread is used as a base for Indian Tacos (recipe on next page) or is sprinkled with powdered sugar and cinnamon or served hot with butter and honey.
Yield: 10-12 fry breads

3 cups flour
2 teaspoons baking powder
1 teaspoon salt
1 ½ cups warm water
1 tablespoon vegetable oil, for

dough, plus more for greasing
your hands
1 cup shortening (such as Crisco)
or vegetable oil, for frying

In a large mixing bowl, stir together the flour, baking powder and salt. Add the water and stir with a large spoon until well-mixed into a sticky dough.

Form dough into a ball; spread 1 tablespoon of oil over the dough. Cover with a dish towel and let stand for about half an hour.

Lightly coat your hands with a little oil and pull off pieces of dough about the size of a tennis ball. Pat each into a circle 5 or 6 inches in diameter, as thin as you can get it. (It helps to make the center thinner than the outside rim.) Add a little more oil to your hands if the dough gets too sticky.

Melt shortening in a heavy skillet over medium-high heat until hot. Fry the dough discs in the hot oil, turning once to brown on each side. Remove to a paper towel to drain. These are best if served immediately.

INDIAN TACOS

Yield: 4-5 servings

1 pound ground beef
1 medium onion, chopped
15-oz. can Ranch Style beans, with liquid (or a 15-oz. can of pinto beans with 1 teaspoon chili powder mixed in)
15-oz. can crushed tomatoes, with liquid

15-oz. can whole-kernel corn, drained
2 teaspoons garlic powder
1 to 2 teaspoons ground cumin, to taste
4 to 5 rounds Indian Fry Bread (see recipe above)

Toppings:
Chopped iceberg lettuce
Chopped tomato
Grated Cheddar cheese

Sour cream, optional
Salsa, optional

Heat a large skillet over medium heat; when hot, add ground beef and chopped onion. Cook, breaking apart the meat as it cooks, until the meat is browned and the onion is tender.

Drain off and discard excess grease, leaving meat in the skillet. Add beans and tomatoes with their liquid, corn, garlic powder and cumin.

Simmer uncovered over low heat about 10 minutes, stirring occasionally, or until the mixture has thickened.

Spoon some of the meat mixture into the center of each fry bread and top with lettuce, tomato and cheese. Garnish with sour cream and/or salsa, if you choose.

POSOLE (PORK AND HOMINY STEW)

Stews are popular in Native American culture because you can add bits of whatever you happen to have on hand. Pork or venison was a staple, and hominy, made from corn, added a hearty element to the dish. For a New Mexico-style native stew, use green chiles instead of green bell pepper.

Yield: 6-8 servings

1 tablespoon vegetable oil
1 to 1 ½ pounds pork shoulder, cut into 1-inch cubes (reserve the bone, if there is one)
1 medium onion, chopped
1 large green bell pepper, chopped, or a 7-oz. can of green chiles
2 (14.5-oz.) cans white hominy, with liquid
14.5-oz. can diced tomatoes, with liquid
2 cloves garlic, peeled and minced
1 teaspoon dried oregano
¼ cup chopped fresh cilantro, optional
Salt and pepper to taste

In a Dutch oven over medium-high heat, heat the oil and brown the pork, turning it to brown evenly. Add the pork bone, if you have one, and stir in onion, bell pepper, hominy, tomatoes and garlic. Bring to a boil; reduce heat to low, cover and simmer for 1 ½ to 2 hours, stirring occasionally, until the meat is tender.

Add the herbs and salt and pepper to taste; simmer, covered, about 30 minutes more.

CHICKEN AND CORN STEW

Yield: 8-10 servings

1 to 2 tablespoons vegetable oil
4 to 6 pieces chicken (breasts or
    thighs work best)
1 large onion, chopped
3 medium potatoes, peeled and
    cut into cubes
Salt and pepper to taste

2 to 3 yellow squash,
    cut into 1-inch cubes
Kernels from 2 to 3 ears of corn,
    cut from the cob, or 2 cups
    frozen corn, defrosted
1 to 2 cloves garlic, peeled and
    minced
1 teaspoon dried oregano

In a large Dutch oven over medium-high heat, heat oil and brown the
chicken pieces on both sides. Add the onion and stir to coat with the oil;
then add the cubed potatoes. Cook, stirring frequently, for several minutes,
until the onion is tender.

Add water to cover the chicken; add salt and pepper to taste. Bring to
a simmer, lower heat to maintain a gentle simmer, cover and simmer for
about 45 minutes, until the chicken is cooked through.

Turn off heat, remove the chicken pieces from the pot and set aside until
chicken is cool enough to pull the meat from the bones. Discard the bones
and return the meat to the pot along with the squash, corn kernels, garlic
and oregano. Simmer, covered, over low heat another 15 to 20 minutes,
until the squash is tender, stirring occasionally. Taste for seasoning and
add more salt and pepper if needed.

FRIED HOMINY

Yield: 4-6 servings

4 strips bacon
½ medium onion, chopped

2 (14.5-oz.) cans white hominy, drained and patted dry
Salt and pepper to taste

In a large skillet, fry bacon over medium-high heat until crisp; remove from pan to drain on paper towels. Add onion to the bacon grease and sauté at the same heat until tender. Add the drained and dried hominy to the onion and stir thoroughly to heat through. Add a healthy amount of black pepper and salt to taste. Crumble the bacon and mix it into the hominy to serve.

FRIED SQUASH PATTIES

Yield: 8-10 patties

2 to 3 yellow squash, diced
1 cup cornmeal
⅓ cup flour
2 eggs, beaten

¼ cup buttermilk
Salt and pepper to taste
1 to 2 tablespoons bacon drippings or vegetable oil

Place squash in a medium saucepan and add just enough water to barely cover the squash. Bring to a boil, then reduce heat and simmer, covered, until the squash is soft. Drain well, discarding liquid, and transfer squash to a mixing bowl to cool.

Add remaining ingredients except for oil to squash and mix well.

Heat the oil in a large skillet over medium-high heat until the oil sizzles robustly when you drop a bit of the squash mixture into the skillet.

Drop large spoonfuls of squash mixture (about ⅓ cup each) into the skillet to form patties. Do not crowd patties; you will need to cook several batches. Fry patties until brown on both sides and drain on paper towels. Serve immediately.

BAKED PUMPKIN

Use small pumpkins for this dish; they are easier to handle than the large ones. Halve each pumpkin and scrape out the seeds and strands inside, using a medium-sized spoon. Cut the pumpkin into large pieces with a large sharp knife. Then slice the peel away from the meat. You can save the pumpkin seeds and roast them to snack on (see recipe below), if you like.

Yield: 3-4 servings

1 small pumpkin, peeled, seeds removed, cut into large cubes
½ stick butter, melted

Pinch salt
1 cup sugar
Powdered cinnamon to taste

Preheat oven to 350°.

Toss the pumpkin in the melted butter with the salt and place cubes in a single layer in a nonstick baking dish. Sprinkle with sugar. Cover with foil and bake until the pumpkin is soft, about 20 to 25 minutes. Sprinkle with cinnamon before serving.

ROASTED PUMPKIN SEEDS

Yield: About 3 cups seeds

Seeds from 1 pumpkin, flesh reserved for other use

2 to 3 tablespoons vegetable oil
Salt to taste

Scrape the pumpkin seeds out of the center of the pumpkin with a spoon, removing all the strands and soft bits of pulp: Separate and discard as much of the strands and soft pulp as you can by hand, then rinse the seeds well in a colander or sieve to remove the rest. Let the seeds dry on a paper towel.

While seeds are drying, preheat oven to 325°.

In a medium bowl, toss the seeds lightly in the vegetable oil. Turn them out onto a cookie sheet and bake until crisp and lightly browned, about 20 minutes. Stir seeds or rotate baking sheet in oven at intervals, if necessary, to make sure they are browning evenly. Remove from oven and sprinkle lightly with salt while still hot.

These will keep for several weeks.

BLACKBERRY FRITTERS

Berries are quite prolific in Texas, and several types can easily be foraged: huckleberries, dewberries and — my favorite — blackberries.
Yield: 15-20 fritters

2 cups blackberries (blueberries, dewberries or huckleberries also can be used)
3 cups flour
½ cup sugar

1 ¼ teaspoons baking powder
3 eggs
½ cup water
3 to 4 tablespoons vegetable oil
Powdered sugar, for serving

Wash berries and spread on paper towels to dry.

In a large mixing bowl, stir together dry ingredients.

In a separate small bowl, beat the eggs with the water until mixture becomes foamy. Mix eggs quickly into dry ingredients. Fold in the berries.

Heat the oil in a skillet over medium-high heat until it is hot enough to sizzle robustly when you drop a bit of the fritter batter into the skillet. Drop large spoonfuls of batter (about ¼ to ⅓ cup each) into the oil and cook until brown on each side, turning once. Sprinkle with powdered sugar and serve immediately.

AFRICAN-AMERICAN TEXANS:
CAST-IRON POTS AND CORNBREAD

IT'S KNOWN AS SOUL FOOD TODAY, but the roots of African-American cuisine in Texas are found in the cultural heritage the early residents brought with them and the limitations they faced in their new home. They ate what they had or what they could find, so it's no surprise their food featured pork, game, fish, vegetables, cornbread and sweet potatoes. The result is a hearty, flavorful food that sticks to your ribs. This style of cooking is particularly entrenched in East Texas, and to make it right, you'll need a seasoned cast-iron skillet, a deep stew pot and a big spoon. You'll also want to stockpile the drippings from a pound or two of bacon, storing the grease in a covered coffee can in your refrigerator, before tackling these recipes. The drippings can keep almost indefinitely.

BLACK-EYED PEAS

Believed to have originated in Africa, black-eyed peas are a staple in African-American cuisine in Texas. They're also a must-have for New Year's Day. For the best results, use fresh peas. If they're in season, you'll often find bags of shucked fresh black-eyed peas at farmers' markets or other stores that sell fresh local produce. Frozen peas are fine, though, and you can also use canned or dried. Served with a side of cornbread and maybe some greens, this will make a substantial meal.

Yield: 10-12 servings

½ bushel fresh black-eyed peas in the hull, or about 6 (14.5-oz.) cans, or 1 ½ pounds dried peas
2 ham hocks (you may also add bits of ham, but be sure to include the bone)

1 medium onion, chopped
1 medium bell pepper, chopped
2 cloves garlic, peeled and minced
Pepper to taste
Salt to taste

For fresh or frozen peas: If peas are still in the shucks, remove the peas from the shucks, adding a few of the smallest and most tender pods whole with the peas still inside (these are known as snaps). Discard the shucks; wash the peas carefully and remove any foreign debris. Place the peas in a stewpot and add water to cover the peas by about 2 inches. Add the ham hocks, cover and bring to a boil. Reduce heat and simmer, covered, about 45 minutes, until peas are tender, stirring occasionally; then follow "Finishing the Peas" instructions.

For canned peas: Empty the peas and their liquid into a stewpot and add water just to cover them. Add the ham hocks, cover and bring to a boil. Reduce heat and simmer, covered, about 30 minutes, until peas are tender, stirring occasionally; then follow "Finishing the Peas" instructions.

For dried peas: Clean and wash the peas, then place in a stewpot. Add enough water just to cover the peas and bring to a boil. Turn off the heat, cover, and let the peas sit for about an hour. Drain the peas, rinse again and then return them to the stewpot. Add the ham hocks and cover with water by about 2 inches. Bring to a boil, reduce heat and simmer, covered, until peas are tender about 45 minutes; then follow "Finishing the Peas" instructions.

Finishing the peas: Once the peas are tender, remove the pot from the heat, pluck out the ham hocks and allow them to cool. Trim or pull the meat off the hocks and add to the peas, discarding any bits of fat. You may also add additional chopped ham, if you like. Add the onion, bell pepper, minced garlic and pepper to the pot, cover and bring to a boil; reduce heat and simmer, covered, for another 20 to 30 minutes, until peas are soft but not mushy. Add salt to taste (for canned peas, you may not need much) and more pepper, if necessary, then push the pot to the back of the stove, leaving the peas covered until you're ready to eat them. Serve with cornbread (recipe on page 23). Many East Texans also like them with a splash of pepper vinegar (made by adding small hot peppers to a bottle of vinegar and letting them marinate in the vinegar) or plain vinegar.

POT O' GREENS

A standard side dish in African-American cooking in Texas, cooked greens can include collard, turnip or mustard greens. For many, a mix of all three — with their slightly different textures and flavors — is best. The key to good greens is to make sure you wash them carefully before you cook them. They tend to hold sand and dirt and can be gritty if you don't wash them well. Many cooks recommend three washes before you ever put them in the pan. If you use salt pork instead of ham hocks, slice it thinly and then soak it in water overnight before using; this will remove some of the salt.

Yield: 6-8 servings

6 to 8 bunches of greens (turnip, collard or mustard greens, or a mix)

2 ham hocks (or about 6 oz. salt pork, sliced and soaked

overnight in water)

1 medium onion, diced

2 to 3 cloves garlic, peeled and minced

Salt and pepper to taste

Wash the greens first: Separate the leaves, place in a large sink or pan and cover with water. Gently stir and agitate the water to loosen any grit that may be on the leaves. Lift each leaf, shaking it gently in the water as you do so, and place into a second container or side sink of clean water. Continue until you have transferred all the leaves into the clean water. Drain the first sink or container and rinse it out. Fill it with clean water and then repeat the process, transferring the leaves from the second sink back into the first sink or pan for the third rinse.

Prepare them for cooking: You'll want to trim off some of the tough stems or ribs that run down the center of the leaf, but there's a bit of a debate over just how much to leave on. Traditionally, only the largest portion of the stem, at the bottom of the leaf, is removed. Some prefer only the tender parts of the leaf, however, and remove the entire stem, which takes longer to cook than the leaves.

To cook: Once you have removed as much of the stem as you like, tear the leaves into large pieces and place into a stewpot. (You'll want the pot to be stuffed to overflowing — these cook down an amazing amount.) Fill the pot about half-full with water (you won't be able to cover the greens) and add the ham hocks, onion, garlic and salt and pepper to taste. Bring the water to a boil, then reduce heat to simmer. Simmer the greens, covered, for about an hour, until tender. Remove the ham hocks and allow them to cool. Trim off the bits of ham to return to the greens; discard the bone and fat. Serve the greens and their liquor with cornbread, passing hot-pepper vinegar on the side.

SKILLET PORK CHOPS AND RED-EYE GRAVY

I can envision a cook with limited resources making breakfast one morning and wanting some gravy to go with the pork chops. A splash of coffee into the skillet and a little boiling, and you have what modern-day chefs would call a reduction.
Yield: 4-6 servings

1 tablespoon bacon drippings (or vegetable oil, but it won't taste the same)	Salt and pepper to taste 4 to 6 thin-sliced pork chops ½ to ¾ cup black coffee

Heat the drippings in a cast-iron skillet over medium-high heat. Salt and pepper the pork chops on each side. Add the pork chops to the hot fat, in batches, if necessary. Cook until the chops are brown on each side and fully cooked, about 5 minutes on each side for very thin pork chops, and transfer them to a plate.

To make the red-eye gravy, maintain the heat under the skillet, add the coffee and stir and scrape to release the bits of meat from the bottom of the skillet. Cook down until the liquid is slightly reduced, stirring constantly. Serve over the pork chops.

SUNDAY FRIED CHICKEN

Fried chicken was served only on special days — usually midday Sunday, after church — because you wouldn't want to deplete your flock of layers. Traditionally, chicken would be fried in a cast-iron skillet, but if you want to minimize the considerable mess to your stove, use a Dutch oven with a lid.
Yield: 6-8 servings

1 whole chicken, cut into pieces
2 cups flour
Salt and pepper to taste
3 eggs

1 ½ cups shortening (such as Crisco) or vegetable oil for frying

Rinse the chicken pieces and pat dry. Put the flour into a large bowl and season with salt and pepper. In a separate bowl, beat the eggs lightly. Melt the shortening in the pan over medium-high heat.

Dip the chicken pieces, one at a time, into the egg and then into the flour, coating it well. When oil is hot enough to sizzle when a little flour is dropped into it, place the chicken gently into the hot oil, starting with the dark-meat pieces. Cook, turning once, until brown on each side, then cover with a lid and cook about 10 minutes. Turn chicken again, cover and cook another 10 minutes or so, until the chicken is fully cooked. Small pieces such as wings will cook more quickly than breasts, and breasts will cook more quickly than thighs, so remove the pieces to a platter as they get done, until all pieces are cooked. You may want to place the cooked chicken on paper towels to absorb any excess oil before serving.

FRIED CHIT'LINS

They're formally known as chitterlings, but they're called chit'lins, and they're the small intestine of a pig. Early Texans had to make the most of every animal they slaughtered, and when they didn't need to make sausage, they made chit'lins. You can find them today in ethnic grocery stores. Word of warning: The boiling process produces a pungent, distinct, permeating smell. But once you fry them — as with many foods — they're good.

Yield: 8-10 servings

5 pounds chitterlings
1 large onion, cut into large slices
1 stalk celery
¼ cup vinegar
2 teaspoons salt
Pepper to taste

2 to 3 eggs, beaten
2 cups cracker crumbs or 1 cup
    cornmeal
1 cup vegetable oil
    (or bacon grease)

Soak the chitterlings in a pot of cold water overnight.

When ready to cook, put a kettle of water on to boil.

Pour off the water from the chitterlings and add the onion, celery and vinegar to the pot, then sprinkle with the salt and pepper. Add boiling water to cover the chitterlings; place pot over low heat; cover and simmer until tender, 30 to 45 minutes.

Drain the chitterlings and let cool; when cool enough to handle, cut them into small pieces.

In a medium mixing bowl, beat the eggs. Put the cracker crumbs or cornmeal in a separate bowl.

Heat the oil in a cast-iron skillet over-medium high-heat until it is hot enough to sizzle when a few cracker crumbs or a few grains of meal are dropped in. Meanwhile, dip the chitterling pieces first into the egg and then into the cracker crumbs. Slide chitterling pieces gently into the skillet and fry until browned, stirring occasionally.

FRIED CATFISH

Catfish are easy to catch in Texas, and easy to cook. You can fry them whole (with the heads cut off) and enjoy the crispy crunch of the fried tail. Or just cook the fillets. They're delicious either way.

Yield: 4 servings

4 whole catfish, cleaned, skinned, heads removed, or 8 catfish filets

1 cup cornmeal

½ cup flour
Salt and pepper to taste
About 1 cup vegetable oil for frying

Rinse the fish, pat dry and set aside.

Combine the cornmeal and flour in a large bowl and stir in salt and black pepper.

Pour about an inch of vegetable oil into a cast-iron skillet and heat it over medium-high heat until the oil sizzles when a bit of meal is dropped into the pan.

Dip the fish into the cornmeal mixture, turning to coat each side, and cook in the hot oil until brown on each side.

COUNTRY SWEET POTATOES

Sweet potatoes can be boiled, mashed, roasted and fried, but one of the best ways to eat them is baked. Early settlers would cook extra potatoes to be eaten cold or used in another recipe the next day.

Yield: 4-6 servings

4 to 6 sweet potatoes

Bacon drippings

Preheat oven to 425°.

Wash each sweet potato and pat dry. Rub each one lightly all over with bacon grease, prick with a fork a few times, then place on a cookie sheet.

Bake the potatoes until the skin loosens and the potato is soft (check for doneness after an hour). Depending on the size of the potatoes, it could take from 1 to 2 hours.

Eat them hot, skins on or peeled (some people like the browned skin, and it is quite nutritious), with butter, salt and pepper or with brown sugar, or leave them to cool overnight with skins on to eat them cold the next day.

SWEET POTATO PATTIES

This is a great use for leftover baked sweet potatoes.
Yield: 4-6 servings

1 to 2 baked sweet potatoes, chilled	2 to 3 tablespoons butter

Peel sweet potatoes and slice crosswise into round slices about ½ inch thick.

Melt the butter in a cast-iron skillet over medium-high heat; when it is fragrant, slide the sweet potato slices into the butter. Cook over medium-high heat until browned on both sides. Serve with salt and pepper or butter and molasses.

FRIED GREEN TOMATOES

There's a point at the end of the season when tomatoes will no longer ripen on the vine, and that's perhaps the best time to cook fried green tomatoes. And while some people prefer to use a cornmeal batter and others prefer only flour, many cooks think a combination of the two works best.
Yield: 6-8 servings

5 to 6 medium to large firm green tomatoes	1 cup cornmeal
1 ½ cups flour	1 cup vegetable oil for frying
	Salt and pepper to taste

Slice the tomatoes very thinly.

In a large bowl, mix the flour and cornmeal together.

In a cast-iron skillet, heat the oil over medium-high heat until the oil sizzles when you add a bit of the flour mixture.

Dip the tomatoes into the flour-cornmeal mixture, turning to coat each side, and slide into the hot oil. Cook over medium-high heat until brown, then turn to brown on the other side. Remove quickly to a paper-towel-lined tray and sprinkle with salt and pepper to taste. These are best when eaten immediately.

OKRA AND TOMATOES

Okra originated in Africa and is easy to grow in Texas, so it was a common ingredient for early African Texans. It can be served as a vegetable — boiled, cooked with tomatoes, sliced thinly and fried with cornmeal — or used as a thickening in soups and stews. This is a favorite recipe.

Yield: 4-6 servings

2 slices bacon
1 medium onion, chopped
15 to 20 small fresh okra pods, cut
 into slices about 1-inch thick
 (about 3 cups sliced okra)

6 to 8 medium tomatoes, chopped
 (or a 14.-5 oz. can of diced
 tomatoes, with liquid)
½ cup water (not necessary if
 using canned tomatoes)
Salt and pepper to taste

Cook the bacon in a large skillet over medium-high heat until crisp. Remove the bacon to drain on paper towels.

Add the onion to the bacon drippings in the skillet and cook, stirring frequently, until tender, lowering heat if necessary to prevent burning. Add the okra, tomatoes and water (if using fresh tomatoes) to the skillet and stir well. Season with salt and pepper; bring to a boil, lower heat to maintain a simmer and cook, covered, for about 15 minutes, or until the okra is tender.

To serve, crumble the bacon and sprinkle it on top of the okra and tomatoes.

TRADITIONAL CORNBREAD

It's a staple in most Southern homes, and this recipe is a favorite.
Yield: 6-8 servings

1 ½ tablespoons bacon grease
1 cup yellow cornmeal
1 cup unbleached flour
    (all-purpose flour is acceptable)
2 to 3 tablespoons sugar, to taste

1 heaping teaspoon baking powder
1 teaspoon salt
¼ teaspoon baking soda
1 egg, beaten
1 cup buttermilk

Set oven to 400°. Put the bacon grease in an 8-inch cast-iron skillet and place the skillet in the oven to heat.

As skillet is heating, combine dry ingredients in a large mixing bowl. Add the egg and buttermilk and mix well with a large spoon.

Once the skillet is heated (it should be almost to the point of smoking), remove it from the oven and pour the batter into the center of the skillet, spreading it evenly out to the sides. The grease in the skillet should be hot enough to sizzle when the batter first makes contact; this will ensure a rich, thick crust. Bake for 20 to 25 minutes, until top is lightly browned, or longer if you prefer a browner, crunchier crust.

CRACKLING BREAD

Cracklings are bits of pigskin that have been deep-fried into crunchy nuggets. Although these pork rinds can be eaten by themselves, salted, and are particularly good with a dash of Tabasco sauce, they are also delicious crumbled and cooked into breads and biscuits. You can usually find them already cooked in Latino markets, where they are known as chicharrones. You can substitute bits of bacon for the cracklings, but they don't have the same flavor.
Yield: 10-12 biscuits

2 cups flour, sifted, plus more for
   rolling out
3 teaspoons baking powder
1 teaspoon sugar
½ teaspoon salt
2 large eggs

⅓ cup buttermilk
3 tablespoons bacon drippings,
   warmed enough to be liquefied
½ cup cracklings or crumbled
   cooked bacon
1 stick (½ cup) melted butter

Sift the dry ingredients together into a large mixing bowl.

In a separate medium bowl, beat the eggs well, then mix the buttermilk into the eggs.

Stir the drippings and the cracklings into the dry ingredients; then gradually stir in the egg mixture, but do not overmix.

Preheat oven to 450° and grease a baking sheet. Lightly flour a bread board and a rolling pin, gather the dough into a ball and roll it out on the board to a thickness of about ¾ inch. With a floured biscuit cutter or clean opened can; cut dough into biscuits about 3 inches across. Place them on the prepared sheet and brush the tops with the melted butter.

Bake 12 to 15 minutes, until golden brown.

For softer biscuits, you can place them next to each other in a greased 9-by-12-inch pan and pull them apart to eat.

PIE CRUST

Pies are a standard dessert in African-American cooking, because they take only a little flour and shortening and a lot of whatever you happen to have on hand: fruit, syrup, vegetables or nuts. Here's a standard recipe for making good pie crust; it will work for cobblers or pies. It's for a single-crust pie, which works with all the pie recipes given here. To speed things up, use the refrigerated pie crusts found in grocery stores — they're surprisingly good.

Yield: 1 pie crust

1 cup flour, plus extra for
   rolling out
½ teaspoon salt

⅓ cup shortening (such as Crisco)
2 tablespoons cold water

Combine flour and salt in a large mixing bowl. Cut the shortening into the flour using a pastry blender or fork until it is the size of small peas. Sprinkle water, a tablespoon at a time, over the flour mixture, tossing and mixing it lightly with a fork until the flour is moistened.

Gather the dough together with your hands and press it into a firm ball. Place dough on a floured bread board or sheet of waxed paper and roll out with a floured rolling pin, starting at the center and rolling outward to the sides. Place in a pie pan, push the crust gently into the bottom of the pan with your fingers so that it conforms snugly to the shape of the pan without leaving any air pockets, then trim the rim of the crust with a paring knife and crimp or flute the rim using a fork or your fingers.

NOTE: For cobblers, make triple this amount.

PEACH COBBLER

Cobblers can be made with just about any fruit. Peach cobbler is perhaps the most popular, as peaches are in such abundance at certain times of the year, though a classic blackberry cobbler is hard to beat.

Yield: 10-12 servings

2 cups sugar, plus more for sprinkling
⅓ cup cornstarch
8 cups sliced fresh peaches (don't use canned peaches; if peaches are out of season, use frozen)
⅔ cup melted butter, divided, plus more for buttering pan
1 teaspoon cinnamon
3 recipes Pie Crust (above), prepared through first paragraph of instructions, or 3 prepackaged refrigerated pie crusts

In a large mixing bowl, combine the sugar and cornstarch. Toss with the peaches, then add ⅓ cup of the melted butter and the cinnamon; mix gently with a wooden spoon until the cornstarch is fully dissolved. Set aside while making the crust.

If you are using the homemade pie crust, divide the dough into two pieces, one slightly larger. Roll out the larger piece on a floured bread board into a rectangle large enough to cover a 9-by-13-inch baking pan. Butter the pan, place the dough in the pan and press it gently into the corners. Roll out the other half for cutting into strips — you will need an equal number of 13-inch and 9-inch strips, all ½ to ¾ inch wide.

If using prepackaged pie crust, butter the pan and line it with 2 of the pie crusts, trimming excess dough from the sides with a paring knife or butter knife and using these pieces to fill in. Patch and pat the dough together so that it covers the entire inside of the pan (don't worry about neatness, since the crust won't be visible under the filling), gently pushing the dough into the corners. Trim the dough square with the edges of the pan. Pour the peach filling into the crust.

Preheat oven to 400°.

Cut the remaining pie crust into long strips and crisscross them on top of the pie to form a lattice. (You can make this simple by first laying all the strips in one direction over the pie, then laying out the strips going perpendicular on top; or you can weave the strips together.) Pinch the ends into the edge of the bottom crust. Brush the top crust with the remaining ⅓ cup of melted butter and sprinkle lightly with sugar. Bake for 30 minutes, or until the crust is lightly browned.

NOTE: For blackberry cobbler, substitute 8 cups of blackberries for the peaches, but stir very gently so as not to break up the delicate berries. Skip the cinnamon.

SWEET POTATO PIE

Yield: 6 servings

2 large sweet potatoes, peeled	1 teaspoon pumpkin pie spice
1 cup sugar	¼ teaspoon salt
⅓ cup butter, softened	⅔ cup evaporated milk
2 eggs	1 unbaked pie shell

Place whole sweet potatoes in a large saucepan and cover with water. Bring to a gentle boil, uncovered, over medium heat, and continue to boil gently until tender (check after 30 minutes by inserting a fork; if the sweet potato is tender, the fork should slide in with no resistance). Drain and allow to cool for about 10 minutes.

Preheat oven to 375°.

Cut the potatoes into 1-inch cubes and place in a large mixing bowl. Beat potatoes with an electric mixer on medium speed about 5 minutes, or until fairly smooth. Stir in sugar and butter, then beat in the eggs, one at a time, and continue beating until smooth. Mix in pie spice, salt and milk. Pour into pie shell and bake for about 70 minutes, or until knife inserted in the center comes out clean. Cool on a wire rack before serving.

PECAN PIE

Dark corn syrup and molasses were used widely in African-American cooking because they were readily available. The dark syrup is one of the reasons pecan pie is so delicious.

Yield: 6 servings

3 large eggs	Dash of salt
1 cup dark corn syrup	1 cup pecan halves
⅔ cup sugar	1 unbaked pie shell
⅓ cup melted butter	

Preheat oven to 350°.

In a large mixing bowl, beat eggs thoroughly with corn syrup, sugar, melted butter and salt. Add pecans, stirring until well distributed. Pour into the pie shell and bake about 50 minutes, or until a knife inserted in the center comes out clean. Allow to cool before serving.

NORWEGIAN TEXANS:
LUTEFISK AND LEFSE

A WAVE OF NORWEGIANS ARRIVED IN TEXAS in the mid-1800s, the result of an active campaign by Norwegian Cleng Peerson to encourage settlers to move to Texas. Most of them settled in Bosque County, northwest of Waco in an area called Norse, near the town of Clifton. Descendants of those first settlers still live in Bosque County and cherish their Norwegian heritage. They celebrate Norwegian Constitution Day (*Syttende Mai,* May 17) every year and throw an annual lutefisk dinner. Lutefisk (LOOT-fisk) is dried cod or ling preserved with lye; it must be reconstituted by being soaked in water before cooking. It's said to be an acquired taste, and turkey and dressing are usually offered as an alternative at the lutefisk dinner.

CODFISH BALLS

This was adapted from a recipe that appeared in "From Norse Kitchens,"
a cookbook issued by the church women of Our Savior's Lutheran Church in
Clifton. The group has been publishing cookbooks since 1960.
Yield: About 50-60 balls

3 cups peeled and diced raw
    potatoes
2 tablespoons butter
1 teaspoon salt
Pepper to taste
1 pound cooked cod fillets, flaked
    (traditional recipes call for a

can of codfish flakes, which are
    no longer widely available)
¼ cup finely minced onion
1 egg
1 cup shortening or vegetable oil
3 to 4 cups finely crushed cracker
    crumbs

In a saucepan, cover diced potatoes with water; cover pan and bring to a boil; reduce heat to a simmer and simmer until tender. Drain potatoes well and mash them thoroughly with a potato masher or large fork, then mix in butter, salt and pepper. Stir in flaked fish and minced onion.

Beat with a spoon or an electric mixer on low speed until fluffy, then beat in the egg.

Shape into golf-ball-sized spheres.

Heat oil in large skillet over medium-high heat until the oil sizzles when you drop in a few cracker crumbs. While oil is heating, spread cracker crumbs in a large plate or on a sheet of waxed paper. Roll each fish ball in cracker crumbs. Fry fish balls in batches — do not crowd the skillet — until golden brown and drain them on paper toweling. Serve hot.

NORWEGIAN MEAT ROLL

This can be sliced and served like lunch meat.
Yield: 10-12 servings

2 ½ pounds beef flank steak	and cut into thin slices
4 tablespoons salt	½ pound pork tenderloin
1 tablespoon black pepper	¼ pound ground beef
1 tablespoon ground ginger	¼ pound ground pork
1 pound round steak, trimmed	½ cup finely minced onion

Trim the fat from the flank steak, place the meat on a work surface, cover with plastic wrap and pound with a meat mallet or other heavy implement it to flatten the steak to about ¼ inch thick, or as thin as you can get it.

In a small bowl, mix the salt, pepper and ginger together and divide the mixture into thirds. Sprinkle the first third onto the flank steak and set the seasoned flank steak aside.

Place the round steak on the work surface, cover with plastic wrap and pound to about ¼ inch thick. Cut into strips about 2 inches wide. Set aside.

Thinly slice the pork tenderloin.

Arrange alternating slices of round steak and pork tenderloin along the length of the flank steak, using all the slices, and sprinkle with another third of the dry seasonings.

In a small bowl, combine the ground pork and ground beef, mixing with your hands, and work in the remaining third of the dry seasonings and the minced onion. Spread the mixture atop the round steak and tenderloin.

Roll up the flank steak tightly, like a jelly roll, and tie the cylinder at intervals with string to keep the stuffing inside. Wrap it tightly in a pastry cloth; place in a Dutch oven and cover with water. Cover Dutch oven and bring the water to a boil, then reduce heat and simmer, covered, on medium-low heat for about 2 hours.

Remove the cloth-wrapped roll from the water and drain, then place on a plate. Cover with another plate, place a heavy weight on top to press out any remaining moisture and set aside. Once the roll has cooled, remove the cloth. Wrap the roll in plastic wrap and refrigerate until ready to serve.

To serve, slice thinly. Serve cold.

LEFSE (POTATO PANCAKES)

This potato pancake recipe was handed down to Jeff Lake of Houston by his Norwegian ancestors.

Yield: 10-12 pancakes

6 to 8 large potatoes (to make 4 cups mashed potatoes)	2 tablespoons sugar, optional
½ cup cream	½ teaspoon salt
⅓ cup butter	2 ½ cups flour, sifted, plus more for flouring

Peel potatoes and cut into chunks, place in a saucepan and cover with water. Cover, bring to a boil, reduce to a simmer and cook, covered, until tender. Drain potatoes thoroughly, then transfer to a large mixing bowl and mash with a potato masher, or put them through a ricer. Measure out 4 cups and save any extra for later use.

Add remaining ingredients except for the flour and beat with a spoon or electric mixer until light. Let the mixture cool to room temperature and then mix in the flour to make a dough.

Turn out the dough onto a lightly floured board or waxed paper. Knead the dough briefly with floured hands and form it into a ball, then shape the ball into a long roll. Cut the roll into portions of about ⅓ cup each and roll each piece into a ball. Working with one ball at a time and adding more flour to the board and to your hands as necessary, flatten the ball with your hands; then, with a lightly floured rolling pin (or, even better, with a rolling pin covered with a pastry cloth) roll it out as thinly as possible.

Heat a griddle or a nonstick skillet over high heat. Add pancakes and cook over high heat for a minute or two, until they bubble a bit and brown spots appear. Turn and brown on the other side.

Serve hot with butter and either brown sugar or salt and pepper.

EASY INSTANT-POTATO LEFSE

This recipe comes from the Norwegian Society of Texas chapter in Clifton, which bills itself as the Norwegian Capital of Texas.
Yield: 10-12 pancakes

4 cups potato flakes	1 ½ cups margarine or butter
4 teaspoons sugar	1 ⅓ cup whole milk
3 teaspoons salt	1 cup half-and-half
3 cups boiling water	1 cup flour, plus more for flouring

Combine dry ingredients in a large mixing bowl.

In a saucepan, combine boiling water, margarine, milk and half-and-half; bring mixture just to a boil. Stir hot mixture into dry ingredients until smooth. Cover and refrigerate overnight.

When you are ready to make the lefse, combine 2 cups of the chilled potato mixture and 1 cup flour. Work together with your hands until the flour has been absorbed; if the dough is too sticky, add more flour.

Place about 1 cup of the dough onto a floured board; using a floured or pastry-cloth-covered rolling pin, roll out as thinly as possible. Cut into rounds with a 4-inch cookie cutter or coffee can. Repeat with remaining dough.

Meanwhile, heat a griddle or nonstick skillet over medium-high heat. Cook as directed in recipe above.

Serve hot with butter and either brown sugar or salt and pepper.

RÖDBETS SALLAD (RED BEET SALAD)

Beets are used throughout Norwegian cooking. This makes a nice salad or side dish.
Yield: 4-6 servings

14.5-oz. can beets
1 large apple, cored and peeled
¼ small onion

½ cup vinegar
1 tablespoon sugar
¼ teaspoon ground allspice

Drain the beets. Chop the beets, apple and onion and place them in a medium mixing bowl. Add vinegar, sugar and allspice and let sit overnight. (You may use canned pickled beets, in which case omit the sugar and vinegar).

NORWEGIAN SWEET AND SOUR CABBAGE

Yield: 6-8 servings

1 head purple cabbage, cored and
    shredded
¼ cup vinegar

2 tablespoons sugar
1 ½ tablespoons caraway seed
1 teaspoon salt

Place cabbage in a large cooking pot and add enough water just to cover the cabbage. Add the remaining ingredients and stir to mix. Cover and bring to a boil; then reduce heat to low. Simmer, covered, on low heat for about 2 hours.

FLATBRØD

This thin, wafer-like flatbread will keep indefinitely and can be used like crackers.
Yield: 20-25 wafers

6 cups flour, plus more for
flouring
2 cups whole-grain wheat flour
(not standard wheat flour)

2 cups cornmeal
2 teaspoons salt
5 cups water

Preheat oven to 350°.

In a large mixing bowl, combine the dry ingredients. Slowly mix in water to form a hard dough. Pinch off a piece about the size of a large egg and use a floured or pastry-cloth-covered rolling pin to roll it out as thinly as possible on a floured work surface. Transfer the rolled-out round onto a baking sheet — Norwegians remove them by rolling them up onto a long wooden stick or dowel, then unrolling them onto the baking sheet. Bake until lightly browned, 8 to 10 minutes. Allow them to cool before serving. Store in a sealed container, as you would crackers.

CHRISTMAS BREAD

This fruitcake-like bread is particularly popular at Christmas.
Yield: 2 loaves

Bread:
4 cups milk
1 cup butter
1 cup sugar
2 (.6-oz.) yeast cakes, or 2 (.25-oz.)
packages of dry yeast
4 cups flour, plus more for
flouring

½ teaspoon ground cardamom
¾ cup raisins
½ cup candied cherries
½ cup chopped pecans
¼ cup citron
½ cup chopped blanched almonds

Icing:
2 cups powdered sugar   ½ teaspoon vanilla (optional)
3 to 4 tablespoons milk

Bread: In a large saucepan over medium-high heat, bring milk almost to a boil, stirring constantly. Watch carefully and remove from heat when you begin to see bubbles.

Stir in the butter and sugar and allow mixture to cool to lukewarm. Add the yeast and stir well. Add the flour and cardamom, mix to form a dough and knead well with floured hands. Place in a large bowl and cover with a dish towel. Let rise in a warm, dry place until doubled in size (this may take up to 2 hours, or less, depending on conditions).

Add all the dried fruit and the nuts and knead again to distribute the fruit and nuts evenly throughout the dough. Cut the dough in half; shape into 2 loaves and place in loaf pans. Preheat oven to 350°. Let the dough rise again until it starts to lift above the pan, then bake for about an hour, until golden brown.

Icing: Mix powdered sugar, milk and vanilla together to form a thick paste and spread it on top of the bread while the bread is still warm.

SANDBAKKELS (BUTTER TARTLETS)

Norwegian Texans are wonderful bakers, and among their favorite pastries are these delicious tartlets. They are baked in special sandbakkel tins, small shallow fluted molds, which can be purchased online; individual tartlet pans could be used as well. This recipe was adapted from one supplied by the Norwegian Society chapter in Clifton.

Yield: About 2 dozen tarts

1 cup butter   1 whole egg plus 1 egg yolk
½ cup shortening (such as Crisco)   1 tablespoon bourbon
2 cups sugar   4 cups flour

In a large bowl with an electric mixer on low speed, blend butter and shortening, then beat in sugar. Add whole egg, egg yolk and bourbon. With beater still running, add flour a little at a time, until the dough leaves the sides of the bowl cleanly and you can handle the dough without it sticking to your hands (you may need to add more flour).

Cover the bowl with plastic wrap and chill the dough in the refrigerator for at least an hour, or overnight, to make it easier to handle.

When ready to make the sandbakkels, preheat oven to 350° and remove dough from refrigerator. Pinch off small pieces of dough and press into the ungreased molds. Place molds on a large cookie sheet and bake for 10 to 11 minutes, or until lightly browned. Cool tartlets in the molds for about 15 minutes, or until the cookies can be removed by turning the molds upside down and gently tapping on the bottom. Store in a tightly sealed container, as you would cookies.

LACE COOKIES

Yield: 15-18 cookies

½ cup flour
½ cup sugar
¼ teaspoon baking powder
½ cup oatmeal

⅓ cup butter, melted
2 tablespoons whipping cream
2 tablespoons light corn syrup
1 tablespoon vanilla

Preheat oven to 375° and lightly grease 2 cookie sheets.

In a large mixing bowl, stir together flour, sugar and baking powder. Add remaining ingredients and mix thoroughly.

Drop dough by large teaspoonfuls about 5 inches apart onto greased cookie sheets. Bake 4 to 6 minutes, or until lightly browned. Let stand 1 minute before removing with a spatula to a wire rack to cool. Repeat the process until you have used up all the dough, cleaning and regreasing the cookie sheets as necessary.

KING HAAKON CAKE

This is named for a much-revered former King of Norway.
Yield: 6-8 servings

3 eggs, lightly beaten
1 ½ cups sugar
1 cup shortening (such as Crisco)
3 cups flour
1 teaspoon baking soda
1 teaspoon baking powder
1 teaspoon ground cinnamon
1 teaspoon ground nutmeg

½ teaspoon salt
1 cup buttermilk
2 tablespoons molasses or dark
   corn syrup
1 cup chopped dates
1 cup chopped pecans
Powdered sugar for topping

Preheat oven to 350°. Grease and flour a 9-by-13-inch baking pan.

Cream together eggs, sugar and shortening in a large mixing bowl.

In a medium mixing bowl, sift flour with baking soda, baking powder, spices and salt. Alternately add this mixture and the buttermilk, a little at a time, to the shortening mixture, mixing after each addition. Stir in syrup, dates and nuts.

Pour batter into prepared pan and bake for 40 to 45 minutes, until a toothpick inserted in the center comes out clean. Sprinkle the top with powdered sugar.

BLOT (LAYERED CAKE)

Yield: 3 cakes, about 12 servings

4 cups flour, plus more for
    flouring
2 teaspoons baking powder
1 cup butter, softened
3 eggs
1 cup sugar
Assorted fillings: vanilla pudding,
jam, sliced strawberries,
    peaches or bananas, pineapple
    chunks, nuts, coconut (any or
    all; your preference)
Whipped cream
Powdered sugar

In a large mixing bowl, mix together flour and baking powder, then cut in the butter with a fork until it is the size of small peas.

In a small mixing bowl, lightly beat the eggs with the sugar, then add to the flour mixture. Knead gently with floured hands until a soft dough is formed.

Preheat oven to 350°.

Divide dough into 9 equal pieces. Flour your rolling pin and your work surface and roll out each piece to about the size of a dinner plate, adding more flour to the rolling pin and the work surface as necessary. Grease as many cookie sheets as you have — you may not be able to bake more than one cake layer on each cookie sheet, so you will have to reuse the cookie sheets until all the layers are baked. Be sure to regrease the sheets each time. Bake each for 10 to 15 minutes, or until lightly browned.

To assemble the cakes, use 3 cake layers per blot, which translates to 2 layers of filling. You can use any combination of fillings between the cake layers — you needn't use all the suggested filling ingredients; choose whatever appeals to your taste — but be sure to cover the top of each layer of filling with whipped cream. Sprinkle the top of the layered cake with powdered sugar and decorate with fruits, nuts or coconut, or all three.

CZECH TEXANS:
KOLACHES AND BUCHTAS

CZECHS BEGAN SETTLING IN TEXAS in the 1800s; by the early 1900s, they had a sizeable population north of Waco in the town of West, which today bills itself as the "Czech Heritage Capital of Texas." Their heritage, food and music are celebrated each year with Westfest on Labor Day Weekend.

BASIC KOLACH DOUGH

In Texas, at least, kolaches are emblematic of the Czech immigrant culture; they're popular for breakfast or as snacks with coffee. They're not just made in Czech bakeries anymore; many a Texas bakery displays tempting rows of these yeast pastries crowned with colorful fruit or cottage-cheese fillings. The basic kolach dough recipe can also be used to make the sausage-filled pigs-in-blankets-like variation known properly as klobasneks (but often lumped with the kolaches in Texas bakeries). This basic kolach dough recipe was provided by the organizers of Westfest and is credited to the late Mrs. E.J. Jerabek. We've included several filling options as well as a streusel topping in the recipes that follow the basic dough recipe.

Yield: About 24 kolaches

2 (.6-oz.) yeast cakes, or 2 (.25-oz.)
  packages dry yeast
¼ cup lukewarm water
  (about 110°)
¾ cup plus 1 teaspoon sugar,
  divided
¾ cup shortening (such as Crisco)
2 egg yolks

2 teaspoons salt
6 cups flour, divided
2 cups milk (or a 14-oz. can of
  evaporated milk plus hot water
  to equal 2 cups)
1 stick (½ cup) butter, melted
1 recipe Kolach Filling (page 40)
1 recipe Posipka Topping (page 41)

Dissolve the yeast in the warm water and sprinkle with 1 teaspoon of the sugar.

While yeast is activating, in a large mixing bowl, use a large spoon to cream together ¾ cup of the sugar and the shortening until light, then add egg yolks and salt, mixing well. Add the water-yeast mixture and about ½ cup of the flour; mix thoroughly with an electric mixer on low speed, or by hand. Mix in the milk; then gradually add the remaining flour, using the mixer or stirring by hand with a wooden spoon until the dough is glossy. Cover and let the dough rise in a warm place until it doubles in size, about an hour.

After the dough has risen, pinch off small portions of the dough about the size of an egg; using a tablespoon, shape into balls and place on 2 large greased baking sheets about an inch apart. Brush the tops with the melted butter. Place the pans in a warm, dry place and let the dough rise until light, about 40 minutes.

(If you are using the cottage cheese filling, you may want to enclose the filling in the kolach dough: Instead of shaping the pieces of dough into balls, pat them out into rough circles, place about a tablespoon of the filling in the center of the circle and pinch all sides together to completely seal. Place sealed-side down on the greased pan and brush with melted butter before setting aside to rise, then sprinkling with topping and baking as instructed below.)

When dough has risen, preheat oven to 425°.

Make an indentation in each piece of dough and place about a tablespoon of fruit or cheese filling into the indentation, dividing the filling evenly among the kolaches. Sprinkle with Posipka Topping and bake for about 15 minutes, until browned. Remove kolaches with a spatula to a wire cooling rack.

KOLACH FILLINGS

Each of these recipes will yield enough for about 24 kolaches.

Cottage cheese filling

1 pint (16 oz.) cottage cheese,
    drained briefly in a sieve
8 oz. cream cheese, at room
    temperature
1 egg yolk

½ cup sugar
Grated rind from one lemon
½ teaspoon lemon flavoring,
    or ¼ teaspoon lemon extract
Pinch of salt

In a medium mixing bowl, thoroughly blend all ingredients. If the mixture seems too loose or moist, gradually mix in a small amount of very finely rolled cracker crumbs to absorb some of the liquid.

Apricot filling

10-oz. package dried apricots   ½ cup sugar, or more to taste

Place the apricots in a saucepan and add enough water just to cover them. Bring to a boil, then reduce heat to low and simmer, uncovered, over low heat until the apricots are soft and most of the water has been absorbed. Do not overcook, or the fruit will turn dark. Add the sugar to taste and stir to dissolve; then mash with a potato masher until the mixture is fairly smooth.

Prune filling

16 oz. pitted prunes
¼ cup sugar

½ teaspoon ground cinnamon

Place the prunes in a saucepan and add enough water just to cover them. Bring to a boil, then reduce heat to low; simmer uncovered over low heat until the prunes are tender and most of the water is absorbed. Add sugar and cinnamon and mix well until the sugar is dissolved. Mash with a potato masher or hand mixer until fairly smooth; don't overmix.

POSIPKA (STREUSEL TOPPING FOR KOLACHES)

Yield: Enough for about 24 kolaches

1 cup sugar
½ cup flour

1 teaspoon cinnamon
2 tablespoons melted butter

In a medium bowl, toss and blend all ingredients together (your hands work well for this) until mixture resembles coarse meal. Sprinkle on top of kolaches before baking.

SAUSAGE AND CHEESE KLOBASNEKS

A klobasnek (derived from the Czech word klobasa, meaning sausage) is similar to a kolach but is filled with link sausage, sometimes with added cheese and/ or sauerkraut. In Texas, jalapeños are often included as well. Most bakeries call these pastries kolaches, but klobasnek is technically correct.
Yield: About 24 pastries

1 recipe Basic Kolach Dough,
    page 38
3 link sausages (German- or
    Polish-style sausage works
    well), each about 6 inches long

16 oz. Cheddar cheese
14.5-oz. can sauerkraut, well-
    drained, OR 2 or 3 jalapeños,
    seeded and chopped finely,
    optional

Prepare the kolach dough through the first rising.

Cut each sausage into 4 pieces, then cut each piece into strips about 3 inches long.

Cut the cheese into strips about ½ inch wide, ½ inch thick and 3 inches long.

Pinch off pieces of the dough about the size of an egg and pat out into rough circles. Place 1 strip each of sausage and cheese in the center of each circle; if desired, top with a little sauerkraut or jalapeño. Wrap the dough around the sausage and other fillings and pinch closed. The dough should completely cover the fillings.

Place klobasneks seam-side down on greased pans and allow to rise.

Preheat oven to 425° and bake klobasneks until browned. Turn out onto a wire rack to cool.

BUCHTAS (FILLED SWEET BUNS)

These filled-and-rolled pastries are similar to kolaches but constructed differently. This recipe was also provided by the Westfest organizers; it is credited to Rose Kubacak.

Yield: 20-22 buns

1 ½ cups milk, lukewarm
¼ cup crumbled yeast cakes, firmly packed
⅓ cup sugar
¼ cup shortening (such as Crisco)
3 egg yolks
1 teaspoon salt

5 ¾ cups flour, plus more for flouring
1 recipe Kolach Filling, your choice of flavor (page 40)
1 recipe Posipka (page 41)
¾ stick (6 tablespoons) butter, melted
Powdered sugar for sprinkling

In a large bowl, mix together the lukewarm milk, crumbled yeast and sugar; let stand until the yeast has dissolved.

In a saucepan over low heat or in a microwave-safe bowl in the microwave, melt the shortening. Let it cool to lukewarm, then add the egg yolks and mix well. Add the shortening-egg mixture to the yeast mixture and stir well, then add salt.

Gradually stir in 2 cups of flour and work dough with a wooden spoon. Gradually add remaining flour, a little at a time, and stir until the dough is glossy. Cover with a dish towel and let stand in a warm place for 20 to 30 minutes. Then work dough down to form a smooth texture on top. Cover again and let stand until the dough has doubled in size.

Lightly flour a board or large sheet of waxed paper and flour a rolling pin.

Grease 2 large baking sheets.

Pull off portions of dough about the size or your fist and place on the floured surface. Roll each piece of dough into a very thin square. Spread your choice of filling over the dough, then sprinkle with the Posipka. Roll each square of dough up as you would a jellyroll. Place on greased pan, seam-side down, and snip the top in several places with scissors or a small paring knife to make small slashes in the dough. Brush the buchtas with melted butter and let rise in a warm place until the dough springs back when touched, about 30 minutes

Preheat oven to 350° degrees; bake for 15 minutes. Allow to cool on the baking sheets. Sprinkle with powdered sugar to serve.

GOULASH

This stew is delicious served with Bread Dumplings (page 00) or over rice or mashed potatoes.

Yield: 8-10 servings

½ cup vegetable oil
2 pounds round steak or pork shoulder, cut into 1- to 2-inch cubes
3 medium onions, chopped
2 cloves garlic, peeled and minced
½ cup flour

6 to 8 medium tomatoes, diced, or 2 (14.5-oz.) cans diced tomatoes
½ cup dark beer
4 teaspoons paprika
Grated zest of 1 lemon
2 teaspoons salt
1/8 teaspoon ground marjoram

In a large Dutch oven, heat the oil over medium-high heat and sear the beef, stirring frequently, until evenly browned. Add the onions and garlic and cook on medium-high until the onions are tender. Add the flour and stir with a wooden spoon to mix well and break up any lumps. Cook, stirring constantly, on medium-high until the flour starts to darken, being careful not to let it burn. Add tomatoes and beer, stir well, then add the remaining ingredients.

Bring the mixture just to a boil, then reduce heat to low. Cover and simmer 1 to 1 ½ hours, until the beef is tender.

TRADITIONAL PORK ROAST

Yield: 8-10 servings

2 tablespoons vegetable oil
2 tablespoons caraway seeds
1 tablespoon prepared mustard
1 tablespoon garlic powder
1 tablespoon salt
2 teaspoons black pepper

5-pound pork shoulder roast
2 large onions, chopped
½ cup beer (preferably dark)
1 tablespoon cornstarch
¼ cup cool water

In a small bowl, stir or whisk together the vegetable oil, caraway, mustard, garlic powder, salt and pepper to form a paste. Rub the paste over the pork roast and let the roast sit for about 30 minutes.

Preheat the oven to 350°. Spread the chopped onions in the bottom of a large roasting pan and pour in the beer. Place the roast on top of the onions and cover the pan with foil. Roast 1 hour, then remove foil and roast another 2 ½ hours. Remove from heat; remove roast from the roasting pan, tent roast with foil and let it sit about 20 minutes before slicing.Meanwhile, to make the gravy, pour the juices and onions from the roasting pan into a saucepan. In a cup, stir the cornstarch into the water until dissolved; add this to the saucepan. Stir over medium heat until the mixture is heated through and beginning to thicken. Serve with the sliced pork.

BREAD DUMPLINGS

These traditional dumplings can be messy to make, but they're worth the trouble. They are a traditional side dish, with stews or meat entrees with gravy.
Yield: 6-8 servings

2 cups flour
1 teaspoon baking powder
1 teaspoon salt

1 egg, lightly beaten
¾ cup lukewarm water
3 slices white bread, cut into cubes

Sift together the flour, baking powder and salt into a large mixing bowl. Mix in the beaten egg, then add the lukewarm water and mix well with a wooden spoon. Add the bread cubes and mix well.

Wet your hands and use them to form the mixture into cylindrical dumplings about 4 to 6 inches long and 4 inches in diameter. Meanwhile, bring a large pot of water to a boil. Drop dumplings gently into the boiling water; reduce heat, cover and cook at a gentle boil 20 to 30 minutes, stirring once, until the dough is firm. Remove the dumplings from the water with a sieve or large slotted spoon, pat dry and slice immediately into 1-inch pieces slices to allow the steam to be released. To serve, top with stew or gravy.

CUCUMBER SALAD

Yield: 6-8 servings

2 medium or large cucumbers,
   peeled
1 medium onion
¼ cup white vinegar
1 teaspoon sugar

1 teaspoon salt
⅓ cup sour cream
1 teaspoon dried dill weed
Paprika to garnish

Slice the cucumbers very thinly. Slice the onion into thin rings, then cut the rings in half to make thin crescents. In a medium mixing bowl, combine the cucumbers, onion, vinegar, sugar and salt. Stir well and then let sit for about 30 minutes, stirring occasionally.

Drain the cucumber mixture thoroughly in a sieve or colander to remove excess moisture. Return to the mixing bowl; add sour cream and dill weed; stir gently until well-mixed. Turn out into a serving dish and sprinkle with paprika. Serve immediately.

CZECH SWEET AND SOUR CABBAGE

Yield: 6-8 servings

1 large head of cabbage
1 medium onion
1 tablespoon bacon drippings or
    shortening (such as Crisco)
1 ½ cups water
½ cup vinegar

½ cup sugar
1 teaspoon salt
½ teaspoon pepper
1 teaspoon caraway seeds
1 tablespoon flour

Shred the cabbage and chop the onion while heating the drippings or shortening in a large skillet over medium-high heat. Set the cabbage aside and add the onion to the skillet and cook, uncovered, stirring frequently, until tender but not brown. Add the water, vinegar, sugar, salt and pepper to the skillet; stir well and bring to a boil. Add the shredded cabbage and the caraway seeds, stirring well to coat the cabbage with the vinegar mixture. Cover and simmer gently for about 30 minutes, until the cabbage is tender. Sprinkle flour over the cabbage and stir until the flour has dissolved. Serve hot.

CABBAGE SOUP

Yield: 8-10 servings

1 or 2 ham hocks
½ head cabbage
2 medium potatoes
2 medium onions
8 to 10 whole peppercorns
¼ teaspoon ground allspice
1 bay leaf

Salt and pepper to taste
2 tablespoons butter
2 tablespoons flour
¼ cup sour cream
2 tablespoons fresh dill or
    1 tablespoon dried dill weed

Place ham hocks in a large Dutch oven and add water just to cover. Bring to a boil over high heat, then reduce heat to low, cover and simmer for about 1 hour. Remove pot from heat, remove the ham hocks from the broth with tongs and set them aside in a bowl to cool. Once they are cool enough to handle, cut the meat off the bone and add the meat back into the broth.

While ham hocks are simmering, shred the cabbage finely, peel and dice the potatoes and chop the onions; set the onions aside for later. When you have returned the meat to the broth, add the cabbage, the potatoes and more water, if needed, to cover. Add peppercorns, allspice, bay leaf and salt and pepper to taste; bring to a boil. Reduce heat so the mixture is just simmering.

In a small skillet, heat the butter over medium-high heat and sauté the chopped onions until tender. Add the flour and cook a few minutes, stirring well to break up any lumps and incorporate the flour. Add about ½ cup of the simmering broth to the onion mixture in the skillet over the heat, stirring well until smooth. Then add all the onion mixture to the soup in the Dutch oven and stir well. Cover and simmer over low heat until the cabbage is tender, about 15 minutes. Taste and add more salt and pepper, if needed.

To serve, stir the sour cream and dill into the soup and cook another few minutes, until heated throughout. Remove the bay leaf and serve.

APPLE STRUDEL

Yield: 8 servings

2 ½ sticks (1 ¼ cup) butter, at
    room temperature, divided
1 cup warm milk
3 cups flour, plus more for rolling
2 egg yolks
Pinch of salt
4 ½ cups sliced apples, peeled,
    cored and diced

1 cup sugar, plus more for
    sprinkling on top
1 teaspoon cinnamon, plus more
    for sprinkling on top
½ cup crushed vanilla wafers
½ cup raisins
½ cup pecans
¼ cup chopped pitted cherries
½ cup flaked coconut, optional

In a large mixing bowl, combine 1 ½ sticks (¾ cup) of the butter, the warm milk, the 3 cups flour, the egg yolks and the salt, stirring until the mixture forms a smooth dough. Divide dough into 4 equal parts, cover or wrap in plastic wrap and chill for 2 or 3 hours, or freeze, tightly wrapped, for later use. (If frozen, allow to thaw at room temperature before using.)

When ready to bake the strudel, melt the remaining 1 stick (½ cup) butter in a small saucepan without boiling. Cover a work surface with a pastry sheet and flour it lightly; flour a rolling pin. Cover a large baking sheet with foil.

Roll out each piece of the dough into a square shape until very thin. Brush each with melted butter. Top each with ¼ of the apples and sprinkle each with ¼ of the sugar and cinnamon. Then sprinkle each with ¼ of the vanilla wafer crumbs, raisins, pecans, cherries and coconut, if using. The filling should not completely cover the dough; leave a small border on each side. Roll up each piece of dough like a jelly roll and place, seam-side down, on the foil-covered baking sheet.

Preheat oven to 350°. Brush the tops of the rolls with the rest of the melted butter and sprinkle with more sugar and cinnamon. Bake for about 1 hour, until golden brown.

MEXICAN TEXANS:
THE ROOTS OF TEX-MEX

THE MELDING OF THE MEXICAN CULTURE with that of the settlers in Texas eventually resulted in a cuisine known as Tex-Mex. It's got plenty of spice (originally used as a preservative) and makes the most out of what was available in South Texas: meat, vegetables, corn and cheese. Today Tex-Mex is a beloved staple of Texas cuisine. The following recipes offer a sampler of some of the most popular Tex-Mex favorites.

BEEF (OR CHICKEN) FAJITAS

These are best cooked on the grill, but you can also cook them on a stovetop. You may prefer to substitute chicken for the beef, preparing it as you would the beef but cooking it a few minutes less on the grill. These are minimalist fajitas, with only bell peppers and onions accompanying the meat; other frequent additions to roll into the tortillas include shredded cheese, sour cream, guacamole or sliced avocados, salsa or pico de gallo, refried beans, chopped tomatoes and chopped or sliced jalapeños.
Yield: 4-5 servings

1 ½ pounds flank steak (also known as skirt steak)
Juice from 2 to 3 large limes
2 cloves garlic, peeled and minced
2 teaspoons ground cumin
Salt and pepper to taste
3 or 4 bell peppers (depending on size), stem and seeds removed, cut in half lengthwise and sliced into crescents (any color will work, but a mix of red and green peppers looks nice)
2 medium onions, sliced into rounds
2 tablespoons vegetable oil
8 to 10 flour tortillas

Sprinkle the flank steak with the lime juice, garlic, cumin, salt and pepper. Cover and set aside to marinate for an hour or so. (For a modern adaptation, mix the minced garlic and the cumin with bottled Italian dressing — skip the lime juice, salt and pepper — and marinate the meat in the dressing).

For grilled fajitas: If you're using a charcoal grill, light the charcoal about a half-hour before serving time so that the coals can burn down to a glowing ash-gray. Spread the charcoal out just before you're ready to cook. If you're using a gas grill, you won't need the extra time for the coals to reach the proper stage; just turn the grill to high.

Drain any liquid off the meat. Cook the meat on the hot grill for 10 to 12 minutes on each side.

Meanwhile, in a large bowl, toss the sliced bell peppers and onions in the vegetable oil and place in a grill basket. Cook on the hot grill, turning the basket once or twice, until tender, about 7 to 10 minutes.

While meat and vegetables are grilling, warm the tortillas: Either heat them about 30 seconds on each side in a hot ungreased skillet, or wrap 4 or 5 tortillas at a time in a damp paper towel and microwave them on high for 1 minute.

Slice the meat into strips and serve with the onions, peppers and hot flour tortillas. Each diner "rolls his own" meat and veggies into the tortillas.

For stovetop fajitas: Drain off any liquid from the marinade and slice the flank steak into strips. Heat the 2 tablespoons vegetable oil in a large skillet over medium-high heat. Add the meat to the oil and cook, turning or tossing to brown evenly, until well-browned on both sides, about 10 to 12 minutes. (If the meat is still tough, cover and cook an extra 10 to 15 minutes, then remove cover and allow the meat to cook another few minutes uncovered before serving, to allow some of the moisture to evaporate.)

Remove the meat to a heated platter and add the onions and peppers to the hot oil. Sauté, stirring or tossing frequently, until tender, about 7 to 10 minutes. Serve the vegetables on the platter with the meat and serve warm flour tortillas alongside for rolling.

Note: If you have a grill pan, you can use it to cook the meat and vegetables on the stovetop as you would over a grill.

CARNE GUISADA

This is delicious served with Mexican rice.
Yield: 4-6 servings

2 tablespoons vegetable oil
½ cup flour
Salt and pepper to taste
2 pounds round steak, cut into
    1-inch cubes
1 bell pepper (any color), chopped

1 medium onion, chopped
1 clove garlic, minced
14.5-oz. can crushed tomatoes,
    with liquid
1 teaspoon ground cumin

Heat the oil in a large skillet over medium-high heat until it sizzles robustly when a little flour is dropped in. While the oil is heating, stir the flour, salt and pepper together in a shallow bowl or plate; toss the steak cubes in the flour, shaking off excess flour, and slide the cubes into the hot oil. Cook, stirring and turning to brown evenly, until brown. Add the bell pepper, onion and garlic and cook, stirring frequently, until the onions are tender. Add the tomatoes and cumin and stir well. Add about ½ cup water and stir. Taste for seasoning and add more salt and/or pepper if needed. Cover and cook about 30 to 45 minutes, until the meat is tender and the sauce has thickened. Serve over rice.

HOMEMADE CHILES RELLENOS

These stuffed chiles are not easy to make, but they're definitely worth the trouble. The secret is in the egg-white batter.
Yield: 6 servings

6 whole poblano peppers
½ pound sharp Cheddar or
    Monterey Jack cheese, grated
6 eggs, separated

½ cup plus 1 tablespoon flour,
    divided
1 teaspoon salt
1 cup corn oil, or more as needed

Set oven temperature on broil to preheat.

Rinse the chiles, put them in a 9-by-13-inch baking dish and place the baking dish on the top rack of the preheated oven. Watch and listen closely (you can leave the oven door ajar to keep an eye on the chiles). When the skins start to make popping sounds and the peppers char and turn black in places, take the dish out of the oven, flip the chiles over with tongs and return to the oven. When both sides are fairly evenly charred, remove the dish from the oven. With tongs, transfer the hot chiles to a sealable plastic bag and seal the bag, allowing them to steam for 5 to 7 minutes, until the outer layer of the skin peels off easily. Remove the charred, shiny outer layer of peel from each chile.

Cut a vertical slit almost the full length of each chile. At the top of the slit, next to the stem, make a small horizontal cut to form a "T." Scrape and pull out the fibers and seeds. Stuff the cleaned interior with the cheese, dividing it among the chiles. Put the stuffed chiles in the refrigerator to chill. Be sure to wash your hands after removing the seeds, and don't touch your eyes.

Whip the egg whites in a large bowl at high speed with an electric mixer until stiff peaks have formed.

In a separate small bowl, beat the egg yolks with 1 tablespoon of the flour and the 1 teaspoon salt. Mix the yolks into the beaten egg whites and stir gently until a paste is formed.

Heat the oil in a large skillet over medium-high heat. Place the remaining ½ cup flour in a shallow medium bowl. Roll each of the stuffed chiles in the flour and then dip each one in the egg batter to coat thickly and evenly. Carefully slide the chiles, seam-side down, into the hot oil and fry, turning once, until both sides are golden brown. Drain briefly on paper towels and serve hot.

ENCHILADAS VERDES (GREEN CHICKEN ENCHILADAS)

These are a great way to use leftover roasted chicken.
Yield: 4-6 servings

2 to 3 cups shredded cooked chicken

2 cups shredded Monterey Jack cheese

4 to 5 teaspoons vegetable oil

12 to 14 fresh corn tortillas

4 (4-oz.) cans chopped green chiles

2 cups sour cream

Spray a 9-by-13-inch baking dish with nonstick cooking spray and place the chicken and the cheese in individual bowls within easy reach.

Heat the vegetable oil over medium heat in a skillet; when oil is hot, slide a corn tortilla into it and cook just briefly, 10 or 15 seconds, until the tortilla is hot and malleable. With tongs, remove the hot tortilla and place it in the prepared baking dish. Working quickly so the tortilla will remain pliable, spread 2 or 3 tablespoons of chicken in the center; sprinkle a little cheese on top of the chicken and quickly fold over the sides to roll up the enchilada. Turn the enchilada seam-side down in the pan. Repeat to assemble the remaining enchiladas, lining them up tightly in the baking dish. Use all the chicken, but leave enough cheese to sprinkle atop the enchiladas when they are ready to bake.

Preheat oven to 400°.

In a medium mixing bowl, mix the green chiles into the sour cream and spread the mixture across the tops of the enchiladas to cover them completely (any corners left uncovered will harden during baking). Sprinkle remaining cheese evenly over the sour cream and bake for about 20 minutes, or until the cheese is melted.

BORRACHO (DRUNKEN) BEANS

Yield: 4-6 servings

2 cups dried pinto beans, or 4 (14.5-oz.) cans of pinto beans

2 cups water

12-oz. bottle of beer (try a dark Mexican beer like Negro Modelo)

1 ham hock or ½ pound ham

1 large onion, cut into large pieces

1 large bell pepper, cut into large pieces

2 cloves garlic, peeled and minced

Salt and pepper to taste

If you're using dried beans, the day before you want to serve them, rinse the beans and remove any debris or stones. Place them in a large pot and add enough water to cover the beans by about 2 inches. Soak the beans overnight.

The next day, drain the beans and place them back in the pot. Add the 2 cups water, the beer and the ham. Cover and bring the pot to a boil, then reduce heat to low and simmer, covered, 2 to 3 hours, stirring occasionally and, toward the end of cooking, checking to see if you need to add water, until the beans are tender.

(If you're using canned beans, omit the 2 cups water; just put the beans with their liquid in the pot with the beer and the ham and bring them to a simmer.)

Add the onion, bell pepper and garlic and simmer, covered, for another 30 minutes. Stir in salt and pepper to taste. Serve the beans with their broth in small bowls.

REFRIED BEANS

You can make these using leftover Borracho Beans or canned pinto beans.
Yield: 4-6 servings

2 to 3 cups cooked pinto beans, or 2 (14.5-oz.) cans pinto beans
4 tablespoons bacon drippings or vegetable oil
1 clove garlic, minced

Salt and pepper to taste
Shredded Monterey Jack cheese and chopped green onions for garnish, optional

Place a colander or sieve over a bowl and drain the beans. Reserve the liquid in the bowl.

Heat the bacon drippings or oil in a large skillet (don't use one whose finish can be damaged by metal implements, as is the case with many nonstick pans) over medium-high heat. Add the drained beans, garlic, salt and pepper to the skillet. Mash the beans with a potato masher or fork, continuing to stir and mash regularly until they are hot and as smooth as possible. If they begin to dry out, add a little of the reserved bean liquid. You can also mash in a little additional oil to make them creamier.

To serve, sprinkle cheese and onions on top, if you like.

MEXICAN RICE

Yield: 6-8 servings

2 tablespoons vegetable oil
2 cups raw long-grain rice
½ medium onion, diced
3 cups water
1 teaspoon salt

1 carrot, peeled and diced into small cubes
½ cup frozen green peas, thawed
2 tablespoons tomato paste

Heat the vegetable oil in a large nonstick skillet over medium-high heat. When the oil is hot, add the dry rice and stir until the rice is well-coated with oil and starts to brown lightly. Add the onion and continue cooking, stirring frequently, until the onion is tender. Add the water and the salt; stir in the carrot cubes, peas and tomato paste. Bring to a boil, then reduce heat to low. Cover and cook at a slow simmer for about 30 minutes, until the rice is tender and the water is absorbed. Uncover and stir occasionally, checking after 20 minutes or so to see if the rice is getting too dry. If the water is absorbed before the rice is tender, add a little more water.

PERFECT GUACAMOLE

The key to great guacamole is a good, ripe avocado. Use Mexican avocados; California avocados have a different texture. To test for ripeness, hold the avocado in the palm of your hand and squeeze very gently — it should feel yielding but not too squishy, with no sunken soft spots.
Yield: 8-10 servings

3 to 4 ripe avocados, depending on size

3 to 4 teaspoons lemon juice, to taste (lime can be substituted)

2 small tomatoes, chopped finely

¼ cup finely chopped onion

¼ cup finely chopped cilantro, optional

1 teaspoon garlic salt

Salt and pepper to taste

Cut each avocado in half and remove the pit (using a teaspoon, scoop around the pit and pop it out). Using a spoon, scoop the flesh out of the peel into a large bowl. Sprinkle the avocado flesh with lemon juice. Mash with a fork or potato masher until creamy.

Gently but thoroughly mix in tomatoes, onion, cilantro (if using), garlic salt and salt and pepper to taste. (You can also add a teaspoon or two of your favorite salsa.) Serve immediately.

SOPAIPILLAS

These puffy fried dough pockets are similar to Native American fry bread. They can be used as a base for savory dishes but are most often served with honey. Some people like to tear off a corner of the sopaipilla and pour in the honey; some like to slather the whole pastry with honey.

Yield: 10-12 sopaipillas

4 cups flour, plus more for flouring

3 tablespoons sugar

3 teaspoons baking powder

1 teaspoon salt

3 tablespoons shortening (such as Crisco)

About 1 cup of milk

1 cup vegetable oil for frying

Powdered sugar for sprinkling, optional

In a large mixing bowl, stir together the flour, sugar, baking powder and salt. Using a pastry cutter or fork, cut the shortening into the flour mixture until you have pieces about the size of small peas. Add just enough milk to make a dough that comes together. Cover and let the bowl stand for about an hour.

Lightly flour a bread board or large sheet of waxed paper; flour a rolling pin and your hands. Roll the dough out on the floured surface to about the thickness of a flour tortilla and cut it into 4-inch squares with a sharp knife.

Heat the oil in a large skillet over medium-high heat. The oil is hot enough when a bit of flour will sizzle robustly when dropped into the oil. Slide the dough squares into the hot oil, a few at a time — do not crowd the skillet; you don't want to cool down the oil. Fry the sopaipillas until brown on both sides; drain briefly on paper toweling and sprinkle with powdered sugar, if desired.

Serve with butter and honey.

EASY TRES LECHES CAKE

This delicious cake takes its name from the three types of milk used in the recipe: sweetened condensed milk, evaporated milk and cream.
Yield: 8-10 servings

18.25-oz. package yellow cake mix (and ingredients needed to bake it)	12-oz. can evaporated milk
	½ cup heavy cream
	Whipped cream (or whipped topping) for topping
14-oz. can sweetened condensed milk	Ground cinnamon for sprinkling

Bake the yellow cake according to instructions in a 9-by-13-inch pan. When cake is browned, remove the pan from the oven and pierce the cake all over with a fork 20 to 30 times. Allow to cool about 30 minutes in the refrigerator.

In a medium mixing bowl, whisk together the three types of milk and slowly pour the mixture over the cooled cake. Refrigerate for at least an hour before topping with whipped cream and sprinkling with cinnamon.

GERMAN TEXANS:
SCHNITZEL AND LEBKUCHEN

German settlers came to Texas in large numbers in the mid-1800s, and many settled in the Texas Hill Country area around New Braunfels and Fredericksburg, where their heritage is alive and well today. Wurstfest in New Braunfels celebrates the music and food of those settlers, as does the Oktoberfest Fredericksburg celebration, and it's the German tradition of smoking meats that we have to thank for the roots of Central Texas' legendary barbecue. Bratwurst, weisswurst and other sausages are a staple of Texas German cuisine, but other traditional foods also have endured.

JAGERSCHNITZEL

This is a German version of Texas chicken fried steak.
Yield: 4-6 servings

4 pork steaks or cutlets	1 medium onion, diced
Salt and pepper to taste	1 cup sliced mushrooms
1 cup bread crumbs	½ cup plus 2 tablespoons cool
1 tablespoon flour	water, divided
1 egg	1 tablespoon cornstarch
1 tablespoon vegetable oil	½ cup sour cream

Lay pork on a flat surface, cover with plastic wrap and pound with a meat mallet or similar heavy implement to a thickness of ¼ to ½ inch. Season with salt and pepper on both sides.

In a wide, shallow bowl, mix together the bread crumbs and flour. In another wide, shallow bowl, lightly beat the egg.

Heat oil in a large skillet over medium-high heat. Preheat your oven to its lowest temperature and place an ovenproof platter in the oven.

While oil is heating, dip the pork steaks into the egg to coat on both sides, then dredge them in the bread crumbs to coat.

When the oil is hot enough to sizzle when a few bread crumbs are dropped into it, lay the pork steaks in the oil and fry until browned on both sides. Don't crowd the steaks; cook them in 2 batches if necessary. Remove the pork to the warmed platter, tent with foil and return platter to the oven to keep the pork warm.

Add onion and mushrooms to the skillet and sauté over medium-high heat, stirring frequently and scraping up any browned bits from the pork, until the onions are just tender and lightly browned. Add ½ cup water to the mixture and stir well; cook, uncovered and stirring occasionally, over medium-high heat about 10 minutes.

Meanwhile, in a cup or small bowl, add cornstarch to the remaining 2 tablespoons of water and mix thoroughly. Add cornstarch mixture to the skillet; stir well. Stir in sour cream and cook until just heated through. Add salt and pepper if needed.

Remove pork from the oven, remove foil and pour sauce over cutlets to serve.

ROULADEN

This stuffed and rolled beef dish can be made in individual-serving-sized rolls (hence the plural form, rouladen), but this recipe makes one big centerpiece roll that looks impressive when sliced. The pickles add a sweet-and-sour element to this dish, one of the better-known in the German repertoire.
Yield: 6-8 servings

1 (1 ½- to 2-pound) round steak
1 ½ tablespoons stone-ground mustard (German-style or brown mustard is best)
Salt and pepper to taste
8-oz. jar dill pickle slices
½ pound thick-sliced bacon
1 cup minced onion

3 to 4 teaspoons capers
2 tablespoons vegetable oil
⅓ cup flour for dredging
2 cups beef broth (or 2 bouillon cubes dissolved in 2 cups water)
2 tablespoons cold water
1 tablespoon cornstarch

Lay the steak out on a work surface, cover with plastic wrap and pound with a meat mallet or other heavy implement until evenly thin, no thicker than ¼ inch. The shape should be roughly square or rectangular. Spread the top surface of the pounded steak with mustard to cover; sprinkle with salt and pepper.

Along the narrowest edge of the beef, leaving a small border at the bottom and on both sides, lay out the dill pickle strips in one horizontal layer the width of the meat. Cover the pickles with the strips of bacon, then top with the onion and capers. Fold both sides over the filling and roll the meat up like a burrito. Tie the roll well with string in several places to hold it together.

In a Dutch oven large enough to hold the rouladen, heat the oil over medium-high heat.

Spread the flour on a sheet of waxed paper and roll the rouladen in the flour to coat. When the oil is hot enough to sizzle robustly if a bit of flour is dropped in, carefully add the rouladen to the skillet and cook, turning, until it is browned all over.

Add the broth to the pot; reduce heat to maintain a simmer, cover and simmer for about 1 ½ hours, turning the rouladen once during cooking.

Transfer rouladen to a serving dish and remove strings. In a small cup or bowl, thoroughly mix together the cold water and the cornstarch. Stir the cornstarch mixture into the broth; raise heat to medium-high and stir the broth until it begins to thicken. Taste sauce to see if it needs salt and pepper. Drizzle some of the sauce over the meat to serve; pour the remaining sauce into a pitcher and pass on the side to be poured over the rouladen when it is sliced and served.

GERMAN POTATO SALAD

Served hot, this potato salad is very different from the mayo-and-mustard potato salad so typical today. So loyal are the adherents to each style that many a family gathering will see both on the dinner table.
Yield: 10-12 servings

6 medium potatoes, unpeeled
2 teaspoons salt, divided
6 to 8 slices bacon
1 medium onion, cut into thin slices
2 tablespoons flour

2 tablespoons sugar
½ teaspoon celery seed
¾ cup water
⅓ cup white vinegar
Pepper to taste

Place potatoes in a large pot, cover them with water and add 1 teaspoon of the salt. Cover and bring the water to a boil; reduce heat to maintain a strong simmer, cover and cook until the potatoes are tender, about 30 minutes. Drain the potatoes and chill them in the refrigerator for 30 to 45 minutes. When cool enough to handle, peel (or leave peel on, if you prefer), slice them as you would a tomato and set them aside.

While potatoes are chilling, in a large skillet, cook the bacon over medium heat until crisp. Remove bacon, leaving drippings in skillet, and drain the bacon on paper toweling.

Add the onion slices to the bacon drippings and sauté over medium heat, stirring frequently, until they are tender.

In a small bowl, mix together the flour, sugar, remaining 1 teaspoon salt and celery seed. Stir this mixture into the cooked onions and continue to cook over medium heat, stirring occasionally, for a few more minutes. Raise heat to high, stir in the water and vinegar, bring to a boil and boil for one minute, stirring constantly.

Reduce heat to medium, gently stir in the sliced potatoes, crumble in the bacon and cook, stirring occasionally, until the potatoes are heated through. Add pepper to taste and serve warm.

RED CABBAGE AND APPLES

Sweet-and-sour cabbage is a staple in German households, and apples — which grow well in the Texas Hill Country — are a natural addition to enhance the flavors.
Yield: 8-10 servings

¼ cup bacon drippings (you can use vegetable oil, but it won't taste the same)
1 medium onion, chopped
2 small apples, peeled, cored and chopped
3 whole cloves
3 tablespoons vinegar (apple cider vinegar would be ideal, but white is fine)
1 large head of red cabbage, cored and shredded
1 ½ cups water
½ teaspoon salt
1 tablespoon sugar

In a large Dutch oven, heat the fat over medium-high heat. Add the onion and cook, stirring frequently, until tender. Add the apples, cloves and vinegar, stirring well to blend. Cover the pan, reduce heat to medium-low and simmer for about 10 minutes.

Add the shredded cabbage and stir well. Add water and salt, bring to a simmer, cover and simmer for about 1 hour, until cabbage is tender. Add sugar, stir well to dissolve, and serve.

KARTOFFELPUFFERS (POTATO PANCAKES)

These are often served hot with applesauce, or with sour cream, salt and pepper.
Yield: 10-12 pancakes

3 medium potatoes, peeled
1 small onion, minced
1 egg, lightly beaten
1 teaspoon salt
½ teaspoon ground nutmeg
¼ teaspoon pepper
1 tablespoon flour
Butter and vegetable oil, for frying

Grate the raw potatoes into a large mixing bowl with the onion, egg, salt, nutmeg and pepper. Sprinkle in the flour and mix well.

Heat 1 tablespoon butter and 1 tablespoon oil in a large skillet over medium heat. For each pancake, scoop up about ¼ cup of potato mixture, tightly packed; form it into a ball with your hands; lay it in the hot oil and press down with a spatula to make a pancake. Repeat, spacing the pancakes so they do not crowd the skillet. Brown on both sides, cooking 5 to 8 minutes on each side, until the potato shreds are tender. Remove to a paper towel.

You will need to cook these in batches, so continue adding butter and vegetable oil to the pan until the pancakes are all cooked. You can keep the cooked pancakes warm in a low oven while you are cooking the rest.

HOT SLAW

The bacon with its drippings and a hefty dose of celery seed add plenty of flavor to this sweet-and-sour slaw, which can be made with either regular green cabbage or red cabbage, or a mix of the two.
Yield: 8-10 servings

1 head cabbage, cored and shredded	crumbled, drippings reserved
½ cup chopped onion	4 eggs
½ cup celery seed	½ cup sugar
Salt to taste	6 tablespoons vinegar
8 slices bacon, fried, drained and	4 heaping teaspoons mayonnaise

Toss the cabbage, onion, celery seed and salt together in a very large bowl. Add the crumbled bacon and the warm bacon drippings and mix well, tossing to coat the cabbage and onion with the drippings.

For the dressing, in a small saucepan, lightly beat the eggs and stir in the sugar and vinegar. Cook, stirring, over low heat until the mixture thickens. Add mayonnaise, stir well and heat through, then pour the hot mixture over the cabbage mixture. Stir well and serve immediately.

LEBKUCHEN

These gingerbread-like cookies are traditionally served at Christmas. Note that you must start these the day before you plan to bake them.

Yield: 20-25 cookies

4 tablespoons molasses
1 pound dark-brown sugar
Finely grated zest of one orange
1 stick (½ cup) butter, cut into several pieces
⅔ cup water
2 tablespoons rye whiskey (or bourbon, which is more common today)

1 ½ teaspoons baking soda
1 teaspoon baking powder
1 teaspoon cinnamon
½ teaspoon ground cloves
½ teaspoon allspice
5 cups flour, plus more for flouring
4 cups pecans or almonds, very finely chopped

In a medium saucepan over medium heat, bring the molasses to a boil; then stir in the brown sugar, orange zest and butter. Reduce heat to low and simmer for several minutes, until the sugar has dissolved. Remove from heat and pour into a large mixing bowl to cool.

When the mixture has cooled, add the water, whiskey, baking soda, baking powder and spices. Stir the 5 cups flour and chopped nuts into the mixture, blending thoroughly. Cover the bowl with a dish towel and let the dough stand overnight on the counter.

In the morning, lightly dust your hands and a board with flour and form the dough into 2 or 3 large rolls 3 to 4 inches in diameter. Chill the dough for at least 2 hours in the refrigerator.

When ready to bake the cookies, preheat oven to 350°. Remove dough from the fridge and cut the rolls into slices about ½ inch thick. Place the slices on nonstick cookie sheets and bake for 12 to 15 minutes.

PFEFFERNUSSEN

The pepper and spices in these cookies add a special bite. The flavors improve if the cookies are allowed to sit for several days; store them in an airtight container.

Yield: 20-25 cookies

4 cups flour
1 teaspoon baking powder
1 teaspoon cinnamon
¾ teaspoon salt
½ teaspoon ground white pepper
½ teaspoon ground cardamom
½ teaspoon ground ginger

1 ¼ cups brown sugar, tightly packed
1 ½ sticks (¾ cup) butter, at room temperature
2 eggs
¾ cup finely chopped almonds

Combine flour, baking powder, cinnamon, salt, white pepper, cardamom and ginger in a medium mixing bowl.

In a separate large mixing bowl, stir the sugar into the butter and beat the mixture until creamy with an electric mixer on medium speed. Add eggs one at a time, beating well after each and stopping periodically to scrape the bowl with a spoon to evenly distribute the ingredients.

Slowly stir the flour-spice mixture and the almonds into the butter-sugar-egg mixture to form a dough.

Preheat oven to 350°. Pinch off bits of dough and roll into 1-inch balls with your hands, placing them on ungreased cookie sheets. Bake for 12 to 14 minutes, until lightly browned.

POLISH TEXANS: PIEROGIS AND KIELBASA

Hundreds of people came from Poland to Texas in the mid-1800s at the urging of Polish priest Leopold Moczygemba. They settled near San Antonio at a place they called Panna Maria, which became the earliest Polish settlement in the entire United States. The settlers there created the state's first Roman Catholic church and its first Polish school. Today, Panna Maria prides itself on its Polish heritage, and residents continue to cook foods from recipes handed down by their ancestors.

BIGOS (POLISH STEW)

This is a hearty traditional dish.
Yield: 12-14 servings

2 slices bacon
1 pound round steak, cut into cubes
1 pound pork shoulder or tenderloin, cut into cubes
1 pound Polish sausage, sliced
Salt and pepper to taste

2 (14.5-oz.) cans sauerkraut, drained and rinsed
1 small head cabbage, cored and chopped
1 cup chopped fresh mushrooms
14.5-oz. can diced tomatoes
1 tablespoon flour

In a Dutch oven over medium heat, fry the bacon until crispy and transfer to paper towels to drain, leaving the drippings. Add the cut-up beef, pork and sausage to the pan and cook over medium-high heat, stirring and turning the meat until it is evenly browned. Add enough water to cover the meat, salt and pepper to taste and bring to a boil. Reduce heat to low, cover and simmer until the beef and pork are tender, about 1 to 1 ½ hours (pork tenderloin will take less time than shoulder to become tender).

Crumble the bacon into the stew and stir in the sauerkraut, cabbage, mushrooms and tomatoes. Add enough water just to cover the meat and vegetables. Bring to a boil, then cover, reduce heat to low and simmer until the cabbage is tender, about another 30 minutes. Sprinkle flour into the stew and stir well. Taste for seasoning.

CABBAGE ROLLS

Yield: 8-10 servings

1 pound ground beef
1 pound ground pork
1 large onion, chopped
2 eggs, lightly beaten
1 cup cooked rice
2 tablespoons dried dill weed
1 teaspoon salt

1 teaspoon pepper
1 head cabbage (look for one with
    large leaves)
1 tablespoon flour
14.5-oz. can tomato sauce
¼ cup milk

Combine beef, pork, onion, eggs, rice, dill weed, salt and pepper in a large mixing bowl; mix thoroughly (use your hands for best results).

Core the cabbage but leave it whole. Bring a large pot of water to a boil and submerge the head of cabbage into the boiling water. As the cabbage starts to soften, remove it from the pot, using two large meat forks or two large slotted spoons, and peel off the softer outer leaves, setting them aside on paper toweling. Return cabbage to the boiling water until the next layer of leaves softens up; repeat until you have all the leaves separated.

Preheat oven to 350° and grease a baking pan large enough to hold all the rolls in a single layer. Spread out a cabbage leaf on a cutting board and place a large spoonful of the meat mixture into the center; wrap the leaf around the meat as you would a burrito, tucking in the ends. Place the roll seam-side down in the greased pan. Continue until all the meat and the larger cabbage leaves are used up, arranging the rolls in a single layer in the pan. Add about ½ inch of water to the pan, cover snugly with a lid or foil and bake for about 1 hour. Remove the pan from the oven, uncover and spoon the juices over the cabbage rolls. Return to the oven, uncovered, and cook another 20 to 30 minutes, until the meat is well done.

To make the sauce, remove the cooked cabbage rolls to a heated platter with tongs and tent with foil to keep warm, leaving the juices in the pan. Pour the juices into a medium saucepan and place over a burner on medium-low heat. Sprinkle in the flour and stir well. Add the tomato sauce and milk and stir well. Taste for seasoning; add more salt and pepper if needed and heat through. Spoon sauce over the rolls to serve.

PIEROGI

These filled dumplings are among the most emblematic of Polish dishes in the United States. We've adapted recipes provided by the Panna Maria Historical Society's "Immaculate Conception Church Anniversary Cookbook" for the basic unleavened dumpling dough and several types of filling. Savory pierogi can be served as appetizer, main dish or side dish; the dumplings can also be stuffed with a sweet filling for dessert.
Yield: About 30-35 pierogi

BASIC DOUGH
2 eggs   **2 teaspoons salt, divided**
**2 cups flour, plus more for
   flouring**

In a large mixing bowl, lightly beat the eggs and stir in the flour and 1 teaspoon of the salt. Add water a little at a time, mixing, until you have a firm dough (it should take only a few teaspoons of water). Flour a large work surface and a rolling pin, divide dough in half and roll the first piece out as thinly as possible (1/8 inch or thinner). Cut into circles about the size of a saucer (you can do this by inverting a saucer onto the dough and tracing around it with the tip of a paring knife, or, if you have an empty can that approximates the size of a saucer, cut the rounds out with the can). Repeat with the second piece of dough.

For each pierog, take a circle of dough and place a spoonful of filling (see recipes below) on half of the circle, leaving room at the edges for crimping. Fold the dough circle over the filling and pinch the edges together to create a seal. If you have difficulty sealing the dough, dab a little water around the bottom edge of each circle to help the dough adhere. Repeat with remaining dough circles and filling.

Fill a large Dutch oven about half full with water, add the remaining 1 teaspoon salt and bring to a boil. Lower the pierogi into the boiling, salted water using a large sieve or slotted spoon and cook about 5 minutes; remove them the same way. You can serve them simply boiled, or you can pat them dry and cook them in butter in a large skillet over medium-high heat until they are browned on each side.

FILLINGS

Sausage: Chop ½ pound of Polish sausage and cook with ½ medium onion, chopped, in a skillet over medium-high heat until the sausage is cooked through. Stir in ¼ cup beer and ½ cup bread crumbs; blend thoroughly; add salt and pepper to taste.

Mushroom: Chop ½ pound mushrooms. In a skillet over medium heat, melt 2 tablespoons of butter and sauté the mushrooms, stirring frequently until tender and lightly browned. Remove from heat and let cool. Mix in 3 tablespoons sour cream, 1 teaspoon dried dill weed or 2 teaspoons fresh; add salt and pepper to taste.

Sauerkraut: Empty a 14.5-oz. can of sauerkraut into a medium saucepan and cook, covered, over medium heat for about 20 minutes, stirring occasionally; then rinse the sauerkraut in cold water and squeeze dry. Meanwhile, chop a small onion; melt 1 teaspoon butter in a skillet over medium heat and sauté the onion until tender. Mix the sauerkraut with the onion; add salt and pepper to taste.

Potato: Peel 3 or 4 medium potatoes and cut into 2-inch chunks. Place in a medium saucepan and cover with water. Add 1 teaspoon salt. Bring the potatoes to a boil, then reduce heat to medium and boil gently until tender, about 8 to 10 minutes. Mash well to make 2 cups. While potatoes are cooking, chop a medium-sized onion; melt 2 tablespoons of butter in a skillet over medium heat and sauté onions until tender. Mix together mashed potatoes, sautéed onion, ½ cup grated Cheddar cheese and salt and pepper to taste.

SAUSAGE AND BEER

Yield: 4 servings

1 pound whole Polish sausage such as kielbasa
6 to 8 small red potatoes, skins on
2 green bell peppers, seeded, cut into strips
1 medium onion, cut into slices
1 ¼ cups beer, about ¾ can (dark beer works especially well)
Salt and pepper to taste

Preheat oven to 350°.

Place sausages in a baking dish and place the vegetables on top. Pour beer over and sprinkle with salt and pepper to taste. Cover with lid or foil and bake for about 30 minutes, stirring occasionally. Uncover and bake another 15 minutes.

BORSCHT

This soup can be served hot or cold and cooked with or without the beet greens. You may want to add a dollop of sour cream just before serving.
Yield: 6-8 servings

1 pound small beets with green tops, or 2 (14.5-oz.) cans sliced beets, with liquid
2 quarts beef broth
2 tablespoons vinegar
2 tablespoons sugar
Salt and pepper to taste

Cut the greens from the beets, rinse the greens thoroughly, trim and chop them. Peel and slice the beets.

In a large Dutch oven, combine the beets and chopped greens with the broth, vinegar and sugar. Bring to a boil over high heat, then reduce heat to low and cover. For fresh beets, simmer about 30 minutes, until beets are tender; for canned beets, about 15 minutes. Remove from heat and taste for seasoning; add salt and pepper if needed. Serve immediately or refrigerate to serve cold. (If serving cold, taste for seasoning again before serving; chilling mutes flavors, and the soup may need more salt and/or pepper.)

SAUERKRAUT SALAD

Sauerkraut is used in all sorts of ways in Polish cooking — as a side dish or as an ingredient in other dishes. This salad is good with sausage or meat.
Yield: 8-10 servings

¼ cup light vegetable oil (such as Canola)
1 tablespoon sugar
1 teaspoon caraway seed
3 (14.5-oz.) cans sauerkraut,
    drained, rinsed and chopped
2 apples, peeled, cored and diced
¾ cup grated carrots
Salt and pepper to taste

In a large bowl, combine oil, sugar and caraway. Stir in sauerkraut. Add apples, carrot and salt and pepper; toss gently. Chill to serve.

PRUNE CAKE

Because of its durability, dried fruit was frequently used in the early days in Texas, particularly in desserts such as this spiced sheet cake.
Yield: 12 servings

16 oz. dried pitted prunes
2 cups flour, plus more for
    flouring pan
1 teaspoon baking soda
1 teaspoon cinnamon
½ teaspoon allspice
½ teaspoon salt
2 ½ cups sugar, divided
¾ cup plus 2 tablespoons butter,
    softened, divided
½ cup plus 3 tablespoons sour
    cream, divided
3 eggs
½ teaspoon vanilla extract
½ cup pecans

In a medium saucepan, cover prunes with enough water to cover by 2 inches. Bring to a boil; then reduce heat to medium-low and simmer, uncovered, for about 15 minutes, until prunes are tender. Drain the prunes and allow to cool. Chop the prunes into small pieces, about the size of peas, and set aside. You should have about 2 cups.

Preheat oven to 350°. Grease and flour a 9-by-13-inch baking pan.

In a medium mixing bowl, stir together the flour, baking soda, cinnamon, allspice and salt.

In a separate large mixing bowl, cream 1 ½ cups of the sugar with ¾ cup of the butter and 3 tablespoons of the sour cream, then add the eggs and 1 cup of the prunes (set aside the rest of the prunes for the icing). Stir with a spoon until well mixed.

Gradually stir the dry ingredients into the prune mixture, mixing well. Pour the batter into the prepared pan. Bake for 30 to 35 minutes, until a toothpick inserted in the center comes out clean. Remove from oven and allow to cool in the baking pan before frosting.

Meanwhile, make the icing: In a medium saucepan, combine the remaining 1 cup cooked prunes, remaining 1 cup sugar, remaining 2 tablespoons butter and remaining ½ cup sour cream. Cook over medium heat for 12 to 15 minutes, stirring frequently. Remove from heat and allow to cool; stir in vanilla and then pecans. Frost the top of the cake with icing.

BUTTERMILK PIE

Yield: 6 servings

4 large eggs, lightly beaten	⅓ cup flour
1 ½ cups sugar	½ teaspoon vanilla extract
1 stick (½ cup) melted butter	Single pie crust, unbaked
½ cup buttermilk	(see recipe on page 24)

Preheat oven to 350°. Combine all ingredients except pie crust in a large bowl and beat with an electric mixer on low speed until smooth. Pour into pie crust and bake about 45 to 50 minutes, until filling is set and lightly browned.

CAJUN TEXANS: PO' BOYS AND GUMBO

These French exiles from Canada's Acadia (now Nova Scotia) first settled in Louisiana before moving into southeast Texas as early as the 1800s. *Les Acadiens*, as they were known before the name was corrupted to "Cajuns," brought with them their unique style of cooking and their fun-loving approach to life, characterized by the popular phrase *"Laissez les bons temps rouler"* ("Let the good times roll"). Their food is based on the things they had at hand — seafood, game, potherbs, rice — pulled together with French flair.

FILÉ GUMBO

The trick to making good gumbo is the roux (pronounced ROO) — the cooked fat-and-flour base that lays the base for everything that comes after. The hardest part is letting it get dark enough without burning it; I usually chicken out before it's quite as dark as I'd like.

Gumbo can be made with any type of seafood — shrimp, oysters, crabmeat, fish — or with chicken or sausage, but I like a combination of them all. Andouille sausage, the aggressively spiced sausage pronounced ahn-DOO-ee by Cajuns, has become so mainstream that most larger supermarkets carry it these days.

Look for the filé — pronounced FEE-lay, a powder made from ground sassa-fras leaves — with the Cajun spices in your grocery store. It's both a flavoring and a thickening agent and should be added at the end of cooking.

This is a very mild gumbo; make sure hot-pepper sauce is available for doctoring it up at the table. Tabasco is the best-known, but I prefer the Louisiana brand for its more balanced flavor and heat profile.

Yield: 8-10 servings

¾ cup plus 2 tablespoons vegetable oil, divided

2 cups chopped raw chicken (chicken tenderloins work well, but thighs or other dark meat add more flavor)

1 large onion, chopped

1 large green bell pepper, chopped

1 cup chopped celery

2 cloves garlic

¾ cup flour

3 (14.5-oz.) cans chicken broth

1 teaspoon salt

1 teaspoon ground black pepper

½ teaspoon dried thyme

½ teaspoon dried oregano

1 bay leaf

1 large andouille sausage, cut into bite-size pieces

1 pound medium-size shrimp, peeled and deveined

1 pint oysters, including their liquid

1 tablespoon filé powder

Cooked white rice for serving

Heat 2 tablespoons of the vegetable oil in a large skillet over medium-high heat. Add the chicken and sear on each side. Add the onion, bell pepper, celery and garlic and cook, stirring frequently, until the vegetables are tender but not browned. Set aside.

In a large Dutch oven, heat the remaining ¾ cup of the oil over medium heat until it is hot but not smoking. Gradually whisk in the flour and cook, whisking constantly, until the roux is a dark brown. Watch very carefully as the roux browns; if you let it burn, you will have to start over. Carefully add the chicken broth, stirring until well-mixed. Add the chicken-and-vegetable mixture, salt, pepper, thyme, oregano and bay leaf, stirring gently. Reduce heat to low, cover and simmer for about 30 minutes.

Stir in the sausage, then the shrimp, then the oysters with their liquid and then the filé; cover and simmer another 20 minutes, until the shrimp is cooked. Serve over white rice in soup bowls. Have hot-pepper sauce and a shaker of filé available for adding at the table.

CRAWFISH OR SHRIMP JAMBALAYA

Like gumbo, jambalaya can be made with a combination of seafood, chicken and sausage, or with all three. I prefer to skip the chicken in jambalaya (it makes more room for the seafood), but it's a great way to use up leftover roasted chicken you may have on hand, so toss it in there if you want. Jambalaya is particularly good with crawfish, those miniature-lobster-like creatures sometimes called "mudbugs" for their propensity for living in shallow waters. The live ones are seasonal, usually available from early spring through early summer, but frozen cooked crawfish tails are widely available at supermarkets, and that's the way you'll probably get them, since it's the tails that are called for in this recipe (both live whole crawfish and crawfish tails are also available online at www.cajungrocer.com or www.lacrawfish.com). Or you can just substitute shrimp.

Yield: 6-8 servings

6 tablespoons bacon drippings or vegetable oil
2 cups uncooked rice
1 large onion, chopped
1 large green bell pepper, chopped
4 stalks celery, chopped
1 pound sausage, cut into bite-size pieces (andouille or another spicy sausage would work well)
14.5-oz. can diced tomatoes, with liquid
2 cloves garlic
1 teaspoon cayenne pepper, or to taste
Salt and pepper to taste
4 cups water
1 pound frozen crawfish tails, thawed, or medium-sized shrimp, peeled and deveined
2 teaspoons filé

In a Dutch oven or a large, deep cast-iron skillet with a lid, heat the bacon drippings over medium heat until hot but not smoking. Add the rice and cook, stirring almost constantly, until it starts to brown. Add the onion, bell pepper and celery; sauté, stirring frequently, until the onions are tender.

Add the sausage, tomatoes with their liquid, garlic, cayenne and salt and pepper to taste; stir well. Slowly add the water to the pot, stirring to blend. Cover and cook over medium-high heat about 20 minutes, then add the crawfish tails or shrimp and the filé. Cover and cook about 20 to 25 minutes more, until the water is absorbed and the rice tender.

Serve with Tabasco or Louisiana brand hot-pepper sauce.

DIRTY RICE

The chicken livers give the rice a "dirty" look but make it taste delicious.
Yield: 6-8 servings

2 tablespoons vegetable oil
1 pound chicken livers, chopped
1 pound mild bulk pork sausage, crumbled
1 cup chopped onion
1 cup chopped green bell pepper
1 cup celery
2 cloves garlic, peeled and minced

2 teaspoons salt
1 ½ cups raw white rice
3 ⅓ cups chicken broth
½ teaspoon cayenne pepper, or to taste
1 or 2 dashes Tabasco or Louisiana brand hot sauce, optional

Heat oil in a large skillet over medium-high heat; add the chicken livers and crumbled sausage and cook, stirring frequently and further breaking up the sausage, until livers are lightly browned, about 5 minutes. Add the onion, bell pepper, celery, garlic and salt to the mixture; cook, stirring often, until the vegetables are tender and the livers are fully cooked, another 5 to 7 minutes.

Add the rice, chicken broth, cayenne and hot sauce (if using) and stir well. Bring to a boil, then reduce heat to low, cover and simmer for about 20 to 25 minutes, until the rice is fully cooked and the liquid has been absorbed. Fluff with a fork before serving, breaking up any large pieces of liver or sausage.

OYSTER PO' BOYS

The first step to making a good po' boy sandwich is frying the oysters. I'm usually tempted just to stop there. But put them on some nice French bread with a spicy remoulade sauce and you've got a meal suitable for rich or poor.
Yield: 4 sandwiches

Slaw:
¾ cup light vegetable oil (canola works well)
¼ cup white vinegar
1 teaspoon sugar
1 teaspoon cayenne pepper
1 teaspoon salt

1 teaspoon granulated garlic
2 cups finely chopped red cabbage
2 cups finely chopped white cabbage
½ cup thinly sliced red onion
½ cup chopped green onions

Remoulade:
¾ cup mayonnaise
2 tablespoons Creole-style or other spicy mustard
2 tablespoons catsup

½ teaspoon cayenne pepper
½ teaspoon prepared horseradish, optional
Salt and black pepper to taste

Oysters:
2 tablespoons butter
1 quart medium-sized oysters, with their liquid
2 eggs
¼ cup milk

2 teaspoons Tabasco or Louisiana brand hot sauce
2 cups cornmeal
2 teaspoons Cajun seasoning
¾ cup vegetable oil

Assembly:
4 hoagie-style bread loaves or French baguettes, split lengthwise

Slaw: In a large mixing bowl, stir together the oil, vinegar, sugar, cayenne, salt and granulated garlic, mixing well. Add the cabbage and the red and green onions; toss well; cover and refrigerate until you are ready to use.

Remoulade: In a medium mixing bowl, stir together all ingredients, mixing well. Cover and refrigerate until ready to serve.

Oysters: Heat the butter over medium-high heat in a large skillet. Drain the oysters in a sieve over a bowl, reserving the liquid, and sauté them in the butter briefly, stirring, just until the edges start to curl. Remove the oysters and drain on paper toweling. Wipe out the skillet.

In a small mixing bowl, lightly beat the eggs and mix in the reserved oyster liquid, the milk and the hot sauce. In a separate bowl, mix the cornmeal and seasoning. Set the bowl with the egg mix and the bowl with the cornmeal next to each other.

Return the skillet to the burner, turn heat to medium-high, add the vegetable oil and heat it until it is very hot but not smoking; a bit of cornmeal should sizzle fiercely when dropped in.

Meanwhile, dip the oysters first in the egg mixture, then in the cornmeal mixture to coat; slide them gently into the hot oil. Don't crowd the skillet; the oysters should not be touching each other. Cook the oysters until they are brown on both sides, turning once, and remove them to drain onto paper toweling.

Assembly: To assemble the sandwiches, spread the inside of the bread with the remoulade sauce, line the oysters up inside and top with the slaw.

RED BEANS AND RICE

Not only can you make these beans ahead of time, but most beans improve when they've had a chance to sit a while to allow the flavors to intensify. Just make the rice and reheat the beans, and you've got supper.

Yield: 6-8 servings

1 pound dried kidney beans
2 tablespoons vegetable oil
1 large onion, chopped
1 large green bell pepper, chopped
1 cup chopped celery
2 cloves garlic, peeled and minced
2 bay leaves
1 teaspoon ground black pepper

1 teaspoon dried thyme
½ teaspoon cayenne pepper
¼ teaspoon dried sage
1 pound andouille sausage
3 or 4 dashes Tabasco or Louisiana
    brand hot sauce
Salt to taste
4 cups hot cooked white rice

Rinse the beans and place them in a large Dutch oven. Cover with water and let soak overnight.

When ready to cook, drain the beans in a colander or large sieve.

Turn a burner to medium-high and heat the Dutch oven until any remaining water has evaporated. Add the oil and heat. Sauté the onion, bell pepper, celery and garlic until the onion is just tender, about 5 minutes. Pour the beans back into the Dutch oven and add just enough water to cover the beans. Stir in the bay leaves, pepper, thyme, cayenne and sage. Bring to a boil, then reduce heat to low and simmer, covered, for about 2 hours. Keep a kettle or pot of water simmering to top off the beans when they need more water; you want to keep them just barely covered with water. Check periodically and give the beans a stir when you do.

When the beans are tender, add the sausage, hot sauce and salt, stir well and cook another 30 minutes. Taste for seasoning and add more salt and/or pepper if needed. Serve the beans over the hot cooked rice.

MAQUE CHOUX

Some people don't use tomatoes in maque choux (pronounced "mock shoe"),
but this is the way I prefer it.
Yield: 6 servings

3 to 4 slices of bacon
¼ to ⅓ cup butter, melted
12 ears corn
1 medium onion, chopped
1 bell pepper (green is traditional,
but use any color), chopped
2 tomatoes, chopped
½ teaspoon cayenne pepper,
optional
Salt and pepper to taste

Cook the bacon in a large skillet over medium-high heat until crisp.
Remove to paper towels to drain; turn off heat. While bacon is cooling,
pour drippings into a measuring cup and add enough melted butter to
make ½ cup; return the mixture to the skillet. Once the bacon is cool,
crumble it into pea-sized pieces.

Cut the corn kernels off the cob into a large bowl, "milking" the juice from
the cobs by scraping downward with the blunt side of the knife. Set aside.

Heat the butter and drippings in the skillet over medium heat; add the
onion, bell pepper and tomatoes and sauté, stirring frequently, until the
onion is tender, about 7 or 8 minutes. Add the corn with its liquid, the
cayenne (if using) and salt and pepper to taste. Cover and cook another
10 to 12 minutes over medium heat, until the corn is tender. Sprinkle with
the crumbled bacon to serve.

BREAD PUDDING WITH WHISKEY SAUCE

Bread pudding originated as a way to use up stale bread. Add a little whiskey sauce and it makes a dessert that's hard to beat.

Yield: 8-10 servings

Bread pudding:

10 to 12 oz. day-old French bread
1 ½ sticks (¾ cup) butter, divided
3 cups milk
¾ cup sugar
1 teaspoon vanilla
1 teaspoon cinnamon
½ teaspoon nutmeg
¼ teaspoon salt
1 cup raisins
3 eggs, lightly beaten
1 cup chopped pecans

Whiskey sauce:

1 ½ cups powdered sugar
2 sticks (1 cup) butter
1 egg
⅓ cup bourbon

Bread pudding:

The day before you make this, tear or cut the French bread up into pieces 1 to 2 inches square, place them in a large bowl and cover with a kitchen towel to allow them to dry out.

When you're ready to make the pudding, use ½ stick (¼ cup) of the butter to grease the sides and bottom of a 9-by-13-inch baking pan. Preheat the oven to 350°.

In a small saucepan, combine the remaining stick (½ cup) butter with the milk, sugar, vanilla, spices and salt. Stir in raisins and cook over medium heat until the butter is melted and the milk is hot but not boiling. Pour the milk mixture over the bread in the bowl. Let sit until the bread is well-soaked and the mixture has cooled a bit, about 10 minutes. Then add the eggs and pecans and stir well.

Pour into the greased baking pan and bake for about an hour to an hour and 15 minutes, until the top is a golden brown. Remove from oven and allow to sit about 15 minutes while you make the whiskey sauce.

Whiskey sauce:

In a small saucepan, combine the powdered sugar and the butter and cook over medium heat until the butter has melted, stirring frequently. Remove from the heat.

In a separate bowl, lightly beat the egg and mix in a bit of the hot butter-sugar mixture to temper the egg. Then gradually whisk the egg into the butter-sugar mixture in the saucepan. Stir in the bourbon. Sauce will thicken as it cools. Serve while the sauce is still warm.

To serve:

Cut the breading pudding into squares, place on dessert plates and drizzle with whiskey sauce.

ETHNIC FESTIVALS

ONE OF THE BEST WAYS TO CELEBRATE Texas' rich cultural heritage is through one of the many festivals held throughout the state. From Native American powwows to German Oktoberfests, Texans turn out in numbers to celebrate and share in the state's ethnic roots. Here is a sampling of ethnic festivals and celebrations throughout Texas.

NATIVE AMERICAN TEXANS

Native American heritage is celebrated throughout Texas with powwow gatherings, presented by inter-tribal associations and featuring tribal dance competitions, arts and crafts, singing and other events. Calendars can be found on several websites, including **www.crazycrow.com**, **www.nativeamericanevents.com** and **www.powwows.com**. The Traders Village flea-market group hosts championship powwows at its extensive open-air market sites in Houston, Grand Prairie and San Antonio, generally in the fall; visit **http://tradersvillage.com**.

AFRICAN-AMERICAN TEXANS

Texans celebrate Juneteenth on and around June 19 to mark the day when the Emancipation Proclamation was first read in Texas—in Galveston, on June 19, 1865, more than two years after it was signed. This was the day African-Americans in Texas realized they were free. Though originally limited to Texas, the Juneteenth tradition has spread beyond the state to become a celebration of freedom throughout the U.S.

Many communities have local celebrations; one of the most extensive is Galveston's two-day celebration, which includes a reading of the proclamation, historical reenactments and a Jubilee picnic. For more info, visit **www.galveston.com/juneteenth/**.

NORWEGIAN TEXANS

Norwegian celebrations abound in Bosque County, in and around the town of Clifton, which bills itself as the "Norwegian Capital of Texas." For more details, go to **www.visitclifton.org**.
—On or around May 17, Clifton celebrates Norwegian Constitution Day, Syttende Mai, with food, music and other cultural treats.
—The Norse Smorgasbord, an elaborate feast served by costumed residents, is held annually in November at Our Savior's Lutheran Church in the Norse Historic District outside Clifton.
—The Norwegian Country Christmas in Clifton is held the first weekend in December and offers a parade, Norwegian and pioneer arts and crafts.
—The annual Lutefisk Dinner, featuring the iconic dried, reconstituted whitefish, is held the first Saturday in December in Cranfills Gap near Clifton. Turkey also served. Etertainers in traditional costumes. For information, visit the Cranfills Gap Lutefisk Dinner page on Facebook.

CZECH TEXANS

Czechs celebrate their heritage with the rousing multi-day celebration known as Westfest, held on Labor Day weekend in the Central Texas town of West, north of Waco. Events include an elaborate parade, the crowning of Miss Westfest, polka music and dancing, a polka mass, sports and family activities, a kolache-baking competition, a taroky (a Czech card game) tournament, craft sales and plenty of Czech food. For more info, visit **www.westfest.com**.

The Texas Czech Heritage and Cultural Center near LaGrange also hosts cultural events: **www.czechtexas.org**.

MEXICAN TEXANS

For some of the most extensive celebrations of Texans' Mexican heritage, head to San Antonio in May or September. Perhaps the best-known celebration is Cinco de Mayo (the Fifth of May), which celebrates the Mexican army's victory over the French in the Battle of Puebla on May 5, 1862. Celebrations are held throughout the state, in communities large and small, but San Antonio's is one of the more elaborate ones.

Don't confuse Cinco de Mayo with Mexican Independence Day, however — that is Sept. 16, known as Diez y Seis de Septiembre. The day that marks Mexico's independence from Spain is also celebrated throughout the state. San Antonio events include a parade, festivals, dancers and other festivities.

For more info, visit **www.visitsanantonio.com**.

GERMAN TEXANS

The quickest way to immerse yourself in German-Texan culture is through one of the state's many Oktoberfest celebrations. One of the best known and most enduring is Wurstfest in New Braunfels, which starts on the Friday before the first Monday in November. Described as a "10-day salute to sausage," the festival includes live music, food, arts and crafts, waltz and polka contests and plenty of beer. For details, visit **www.wurstfest.com**.

The nearby Hill Country town of Fredericksburg, which also has a strong German heritage, is now giving New Braunfels a run for its money with Oktoberfest Fredericksburg celebrations in early October. Attractions include oompah bands and other German music, food, crafts, games, children's activities and a German Bier Tent. It is generally held in early October. Details: **www.oktoberfestinfbg.com**.

POLISH TEXANS

Polish Texans and others celebrate the Dozynki Polish Harvest Festival in September in Houston, traditionally marking the end of harvest for farmers. The celebration includes food, folk dancing and live music. Several other Texas communities, including Bremond and Chappell Hill, also host Polish celebrations; for more details, visit **www.polish-texans.com**.

CAJUN TEXANS

No event celebrates the Cajun culture like Mardi Gras, or Fat Tuesday, the day before Ash Wednesday. And no place in Texas celebrates Mardi Gras like Galveston. It's as close to a New Orleans celebration as you'll find, with more than a week of parades, concerts, parties, balls and other events — and plenty of those Mardi Gras beads. Info: **www.mardigrasgalveston.com**.

INDEX

BREADS, PASTRIES AND COOKIES

DESSERTS

MAIN DISHES

Beef (or Chicken) Fajitas 49
Bigos (Polish Stew) 66
Black-Eyed Peas 14
Borracho (Drunken) Beans 53
Cabbage Rolls 67
Carne Guisada 51
Chicken and Corn Stew 10
Codfish Balls 28
Crawfish or Shrimp Jambalaya 75
Dirty Rice 76
Enchiladas Verdes
   (Green Chicken Enchiladas) 52
Filé Gumbo 73
Fried Catfish 20
Goulash 43

Homemade Chiles Rellenos 51
Indian Tacos 8
Jagerschnitzel 58
Norwegian Meat Roll 29
Oyster Po' Boys 77
Pierogi 68
Posole (Pork and Hominy Stew) 9
Red Beans and Rice 79
Rouladen 59
Sausage and Beer 70
Skillet Pork Chops and Red-Eye
   Gravy 17
Sunday Fried Chicken 18
Traditional Pork Roast 44

SALADS

Cucumber Salad 45
German Potato Salad 61
Hot Slaw 63

Rödbets Sallad (Red Beet Salad) 32
Sauerkraut Salad 71

SNACKS AND APPETIZERS

Borscht 70
Codfish Balls 28
Flatbrød 33
Fried Chit'lins 19
Kartoffelpuffers
   (Potato Pancakes) 62

Perfect Guacamole 55
Pierogi 68
Roasted Pumpkin Seeds 12
Sausage and Cheese Klobasneks 41

SOUPS AND STEWS

VEGETABLES AND OTHER SIDE DISHES